The Power

of Five

Women Who Lead, Lift, and Inspire!

Promoted by Grace!

Dr. Kyshone C. Moss

Attention: Permissions Coordinator

Welcome To The Storm Publishing!
info@w2tspublishing.net

Ordering Information:
Quantity sales. Special discounts are available on quantity purchases by corporations, associations, and others. For details, contact the publisher at the email address above.

Orders by U.S. trade bookstores and wholesalers.

ISBN: 978-1-966612-63-6

Cover Design: Kasper Harris of Gifft Grafix

Veronica Miller, Red Diamond Editing by V. Rena

First Printed Edition: October 2025

Printed in the United States of America

To my soror bestie, Kyshone,

Reading your story and seeing your heart poured into *Our Power – The Anthology, Volume 3* has been such a gift. From sisterhood to laughter, to lifting each other through challenges, you embody the true meaning of friendship and Delta love. I'm so proud of the light you bring to the world and honored to celebrate this milestone with you.

With sisterly love always,

Kebra

CONTENTS

Dr. Kyshone C. Moss

Author
Woman of God
Founder of RestoreHERR
Registered Nurse

Promoted by Grace!

Fresh New Beginnings

In the summer of 2015, I uprooted my family and moved from El Paso, Texas, to Coppell, Texas. Starting fresh in the suburbs wasn't about leaving the past behind—it was about choosing to live life at a different pace.

I began a new corporate job as a manager, a shift after ten years of working with the military. The company was well-established in another region but new to this area. I had to put my nursing skills to use and build a team from the ground up. That meant hiring nurses, social workers, and non-clinical staff. It was an exciting new career path, full of possibilities.

On my first day, I stood in front of the mirror, adjusted my blazer, and reminded myself that I belonged. My heart raced as I walked into the glass building, but I held my head high. The office buzzed with energy and the movement of unfamiliar faces.

Each day, the whispers of doubt grew quieter while confidence began to take root. I discovered favorite food spots, learned the quickest highway routes, and felt a gradual shift from outsider to belonging. I made mistakes, asked questions, laughed too loudly in meetings, and stayed up too late unpacking one last box. Life was slowly unfolding—in this new place, and in this new version of myself.

I realized that new beginnings weren't loud. They didn't always arrive with fireworks or fanfare. Sometimes, they came with a rain-soaked welcome and a second sunrise. And sometimes, they started with a single step in a new direction.

I began attending meetings with medical staff, making major decisions, implementing programs and processes, and writing training curricula alongside the education team. Before long, I was selected for large-scale projects—developing workflows and audit tools that would eventually be adopted across other regions of the company.

I collaborated with different departments to find ways we could better support one another in providing daily patient care. Together, we created reporting systems that ensured providers understood what was expected of them—and how they were performing.

It was a strong start to my new career path, and I felt empowered. I realized that new beginnings weren't always about grand plans. Sometimes, they came in the form of saying yes to the quiet invitation of change.

Overachiever

My boss gave me the freedom to work with autonomy, and I began to flourish within the company. Each month, I reviewed my job description to ensure I was fulfilling every responsibility—including the inevitable "additional duties as assigned." I didn't want to overlook anything or give anyone a reason to question my dedication.

One requirement stood out: the job description clearly stated that I needed to obtain my Case Management Certification within twelve months of employment. Determined not to fall behind or risk any doubt about my commitment, I applied early, immersed myself in study materials, and pushed myself to learn every detail that might appear on the exam.

When the day of the exam arrived, I was nervous but prepared. Passing it became one of the proudest moments of my professional life. It wasn't just a certification—it was proof that I was marketable in the case management community. It validated my skills and gave me the confidence to aim even higher.

With that momentum, I enrolled in every leadership course I could find.

I wanted to sharpen my skills, expand my network, and establish myself as a leader. Quietly, another goal began to take shape: I started asking about pathways to pursue my Doctorate of Nursing Practice. I wanted to be a trailblazer, to rise to the top of my leadership cohort—not for recognition, but for the knowledge, the credibility, and the example I could set.

Still, this was a personal dream I chose to nurture in silence. I researched programs, contacted admissions offices, and mapped out what it would take—but I told no one, not even those closest to me at work. Some dreams need space to grow before they are shared.

At the same time, I made a conscious decision to deepen my understanding of this new side of nursing. When I visited providers' offices, I wanted to be more than just a familiar face—I wanted to be a resource. I worked hard to gain the knowledge to answer their questions, and when I didn't have an answer, I made it my mission to find one. I always followed up, making sure no question went unanswered.

Along the way, I discovered a difficult but necessary truth: when you share your goals, not everyone will be happy for you. Sometimes, the very people you expect to celebrate with you respond instead with silence, skepticism, or subtle resistance. I had to learn that the hard way. Still, I pressed forward quietly and with determination, reminding myself that not every path comes with applause—sometimes, it simply requires perseverance.

The Enemy

It didn't take long for me to realize that my new boss wasn't just difficult—she was deliberate.

On my first day, she arrived early, full of ambition and armed with a list of ideas. I had moved across the state for this job, drawn by promises of growth and leadership. But within two months, the tone had already shifted.

My boss and co-manager rarely spoke face-to-face. Instead, they relied on clipped emails—except when she needed to correct me or ask me to cover a meeting. At first, I told myself it was because our company was new to the area, and that these were simply growing pains—common enough in upper management. But when she began taking credit for my work in meetings, the situation became clear.

She never highlighted our department's accomplishments in Executive Leadership meetings. Instead, senior leaders would approach me directly, asking about our progress, because she downplayed our work—saying we were "just completing the tasks at hand." What made it worse was that she never allowed managers to attend those meetings—not even as observers.

Another red flag was her refusal to share the organization chart. To this day, I don't understand why it was treated as a secret. This wasn't mentorship—it was control.

The pattern became even clearer when my co-manager was promoted. Suddenly, I had two leaders I found difficult, and the environment grew increasingly toxic.

My new boss began giving vague instructions—assigning tasks with little context—while steadily shifting her entire workload onto me. She scheduled meetings that had once been hers but now included me, and I was suddenly expected to lead them. She'd casually ask, "Can you take this on?" or "Could you handle that?"—and then criticize me for "having too much on my plate."

I made sure to be on time for every meeting. My reports were thorough, and I took pride in producing quality work. But she disliked when others recognized me. More than once, I brought new workflows or processes to her during our weekly one-on-one meetings, only to watch her present them to leadership as her own—without any acknowledgment of my role. And when I tried to advocate for myself, she would make slick remarks while pretending to support me.

The worst part? I wasn't the only one. Others from her previous department had similar stories. She had been transferred to our team because she was on the verge of being fired in her old one—an exit arranged before HR could act. Since our department was new, leadership may not have known her history. But behind closed doors, she operated with calculated secrecy—and, in truth, with cruelty.

Then came an opportunity for me to be promoted to the next level. I had been with the company from the very beginning, met our goals, received strong reviews, and achieved numerous accomplishments. I applied and interviewed for the position, and after each conversation with the executives, I felt increasingly confident. Before long, I was the final candidate left in the running.

But soon, delays started piling up. I waited unusually long to hear back from the recruiter. Even the executives asked when I would be starting—they were under the impression that the decision had already been made. That's when I discovered the truth: my leader had canceled the position.

And not just once—this happened twice.

I began to feel undervalued, betrayed, unworthy, and, frankly, angry. Still, I continued to do my job, even though I knew the truth behind the canceled promotions.

During this time, I also launched a new process that required hiring additional leaders and staff. I thought this would finally be my opportunity to move forward. But once again—disappointment.

The weight of it all grew heavier. I shared my frustrations with my mentor, who lived in another city. Many nights, I called her just to talk, seeking advice and perspective. She listened carefully and promised she would look into the situation herself.

The stress soon became unbearable. I started getting physically sick every day I walked into the building. My leader was blatantly unfair and showed clear favoritism. Other managers were allowed to work from home, but whenever I asked, it was always met with resistance—and an attitude.

One manager, in particular, never finished her projects, ignored emails, and often showed up to work looking as if she had just rolled out of bed. Yet she faced no consequences.

I swallowed my pride, stayed quiet, and prayed. The atmosphere in that office was heavy—charged with hostility and resentment. At times, I cried because I truly loved my job and my employees. I couldn't believe the treatment I was receiving.

Eventually, I gathered the courage to share my experience with a few trusted women leaders. They listened closely and offered sound advice. They were shocked—stunned that this was happening to me.

They asked how I had managed to keep my composure through it all. I told them simply: "By the grace of God."

GOD's GRACE and MERCY

I began to pray more and more. "God, please remove me from this place of torture and lead me to a place of peace."

I prayed constantly, but God always responded gently: "Daughter, I hear you. I got you."

With those words in my heart, I tried to tune out the rudeness and negativity that surrounded me. I focused on the work, on the good, on the future I believed was coming.

In April of 2019, I had back surgery, which gave me some much-needed time away from the chaos. During my absence, my boss had no choice but to manage the team herself. For years, I had been the one handling most of the work—audits, reports, and representing our team.

When I returned, she acted more cordial—for a while. I knew why. She had finally seen firsthand how much I carried on my shoulders every single day.

I told myself I would focus only on the positive moving forward. Every day, I made it a point to visit other floors and sections to talk with teammates and collaborate. Doing so kept me current on updates and helped me better prepare my team for success. We had to work together, and I leaned on my gift—networking. Day after day, I built those connections. I didn't expose myself to the negativity. I refused to give it space in my life.

Then, one October night in 2019, around 10 p.m., I received a text message:

"I have a job offer for you in Houston."

I stared at the screen in disbelief. I texted back: "I just bought my home. I can't uproot my family."

They replied, "You don't have to move. You'll just need to travel every so often."

I said, "Let's chat tomorrow so I can fully understand what's going on."

That night, I praised God. He had heard my cry!

The next day, I received a call from the recruiter. She explained that as they were wrapping up a recruiting event in Houston, my name had come up in conversation on their way back. They needed someone with experience to help launch a new expansion for the company in Houston.

I was elated—my name was being discussed in a room I had never even stepped into. I knew it was all God.

The following day, I officially applied for the job. Then, I waited for the recruiter's call.

Company policy required employees pursuing another internal position—whether a promotion or a lateral move—to inform their current boss. My intentions were already clear. I had applied for promotions three times before, and it was documented. I was covered.

A few days later—maybe a week—I received the call on my way home. It was the recruiter.

"You've been selected for the position. Do you want to accept?"

"Yes!" I said without hesitation.

As soon as I hung up, I called my boss. "I need to talk to you," I told her.

I reminded her that I had always been transparent about my eagerness to grow and my intent to seek new opportunities. Then I said it plainly:

"I am transferring to another region to build a new department from scratch."

Silence. You could have heard a pin drop on the carpet in her office.

Finally, she said, "Congratulations."

"Thank you," I replied—and I hung up. Then I praised God all the way home.

Normally, as a leader, you were expected to stay for thirty days before moving into a new role. But do you know they tried to make me stay until February of 2020? It was only November 2019! They were furious, scrambling to keep me.

"You're our best manager. We were trying to develop you," they claimed.

But my mentor had already done her research—and they had to answer to her. She asked them bluntly:

"What development does she need? She is already qualified for this position."

They seemed to forget that I held a Master's in Nursing and a Case Management Certification. I had a higher degree than my own boss. They tried everything to make me stay. I just walked into that office each day with a smile. Oh yes—they even tried to take away my remote workdays. But God was already moving. I was finally released two weeks before my official report date. I left that place with my dignity, my sanity, and the favor of God covering me.

In my new region, I flourished. I rose quickly in my role, and after only a year and a half, I was promoted to the next level—without an interview, without even applying. Once again, my name was being mentioned in rooms I had never stepped into. And that promotion? It brought me right back to my old region. God truly prepared a table before me in the presence of my enemies.

I walked back through those doors—and there she was. My old boss, on her way out of the company. **BOOM.**

Favor

For years, I woke up with a knot in my chest and a heavy sense of anxiety.

My job had once felt like a calling. I believed in the mission, the people, the work. But when leadership changed course, everything good was swept away.

In those moments, I held on to a verse from my Christian upbringing:

"He gives beauty for ashes, strength for fear, gladness for mourning, peace for despair."

Over the next few weeks, I began to heal—not through a sudden breakthrough, but through small graces: a kind note from a former coworker I had left behind, a sincere word of appreciation from my new leader, and quiet moments of stillness where my soul could finally exhale.

God's grace didn't erase what had happened, but it transformed how I carried it. My pain became part of my testimony, not a weight. In time, a new door opened—not just to a paycheck, but to a renewed sense of purpose.

This new job wasn't glamorous, but it was good. It was built on healthy leadership, real teamwork, and genuine respect. For the first time in a long while, I no longer felt the need to prove my worth—I had already been redeemed by something greater than office politics and mean-spirited games.

I had walked through the fire, but I hadn't walked alone. From the ashes, grace rebuilt my life.

For the first time in years, I felt valued. My work spoke for itself. The projects I implemented brought recognition, and I finally had a voice.

My new boss wasn't condescending. She respected me, and I respected her. She gave me autonomy, trusted me to learn, and took the time to show me the ropes. When I made mistakes, she didn't shame me. Instead, she asked, "How can you turn it around?"

She pulled me toward my full potential—and beyond.

When she saw me struggling, she didn't scold me—she mentored me. She gave me space to grow, to refine my skills. And when I thought I had nothing left to give, she pushed me to the edge of my own limits—and I discovered I could go further.

Slowly, I began to see myself differently. I was no longer the broken woman who had walked out of that toxic office months before. I was becoming a leader again—one who led with both heart and purpose.

Over time, I took on a large share of the section's projects and became a key contributor to one of the largest hospital groups in the system. They had struggled for years to get support from my side of the table. I changed that. I built bridges, fostered collaboration, and together we made real progress as a unified team.

The work wasn't easy. It was demanding, sometimes exhausting—but this time, it was deeply fulfilling. I was seen. I was heard.

During my time at this company, I've been honored with three High Achiever Awards, Nurse of the Quarter, and two Leadership Awards.

But the greatest milestone? I was promoted to Vice President of my department—and my boss was promoted as well. We celebrated each other's wins, something I had never experienced before in leadership.

About a year earlier, one of my good friends had told me:

"Dr. Moss, she's grooming you to take her position."

At the time, I brushed it off. I thought, No, she's not. She just wants me to be the best I can be at this level.

I never imagined that a young, educated Black woman from Gary, Indiana—with a Doctorate in Nursing—could rise once again to an even higher position. Not because I doubted God, but because I had learned not to place too much trust in people.

People will fail you every time—but God will always remain by your side.

"The Lord is close to the brokenhearted and saves those who are crushed in spirit." —Psalm 34:18

And I was living proof of that promise.

About the Author

Dr. Kyshone C. Moss is a best-selling author renowned for her debut book, *Joy 365*, an anthology featuring contributions from 364 other authors. She wrote her first book, *From Dreams to Life to Restoration! A Woman's Journey with GOD*. An alumna of Indiana University Northwest in Gary, Indiana, Kyshone now resides in Texas.

With over 20 years of experience in nursing, her professional background complements her passion for writing, which began in earnest with journaling in 2017. Kyshone's journaling was set aside for several years until a divine inspiration led her to share her writings. Driven by a deep commitment to uplifting and encouraging others, she uses her platform to offer hope—even in challenging times.

Dr. Kyshone C. Moss joined her current organization in 2015 and now serves as the Vice President of Care and Value for the Houston/North Texas Region. Her career began within the Care Management department and has steadily advanced over the past four years. Her purview includes oversight of the Houston/North Texas Strategic Partnership Team, the North Texas Facility Care Model Hospital Team, and the North Texas Hospital Partnerships.

She brings more than two decades of experience in nursing, quality improvement, and medical management. Kyshone holds a Doctorate of Nursing Practice degree from South University and a board certification in Case Management.

Her responsibilities encompass overseeing Care and Value initiatives for both the Strategic Partnership Team and Facility Care Model Teams in North Texas. She works collaboratively with her Matrix Physician Dyad to bridge Care and Value efforts across all disciplines—facilitating and enhancing better patient outcomes and experiences.

Kyshone is happily married to her wonderful husband and is the proud mother of three handsome sons. Born in Hammond and raised in Gary, Indiana, she has been an active member of Delta Sigma Theta Sorority, Inc. for 27 years. She is also a devoted member of Antioch Christian Church in Irving, Texas, a community dedicated to reflecting the teachings of Jesus.

In her free time, Kyshone cherishes family moments and stays connected with friends. She strives each day to bless and encourage at least one person, embodying her lifelong commitment to making a positive impact.

How to Connect with Dr. Kyshone:

LinkedIn: Kyshone Moss, DNP, RN, CMGT-BC

Facebook: @Dr. Kyshone Tyner Moss

Instagram: @drchaychay2018

Acknowledgements

I dedicate this book to **GOD ALMIGHTY**—the Author and Finisher of my faith. You are the reason I am still here, standing, and able to be a blessing to others. You allowed me to grow through trials and tribulations in my career, and through each obstacle, You strengthened me. Thank You for using my life as an example of Your grace, Your power, and Your unending love.

To my husband, Dennis Jr., and my sons, Dantrell, Dianta, and Dennis III—you are my heart. I thank God every day for the gift of doing life with you. Thank you for pushing me, for believing in me, for cheering me on when I needed it most. Your love, your encouragement, and your unwavering support mean more to me than words can say. I love you—always and forever.

Tameka Citchen-Spruce

Producer, Speaker and Disability Justice Activist at Living
Unapologetically Media
Independent Film Producer and Screenwriter
Disability Justice Activist
Motivational Speaker
Film Producer

From "No" to "Yes"- A Black Disabled Woman's Leadership Journey!

Introduction

Growing up as a chocolate-brown African American girl who used a wheelchair, I often felt like I was caught in a storm of rejection. The word *"no"* echoed around me constantly.

No—the boys I liked in junior high and high school never liked me back. And when one finally did in ninth grade, he later admitted he only dated me because he felt sorry for me. Why? You guessed it—because of my disability.

No—I couldn't be a model, even though a modeling agent once told me

I had a great look and was "cute." But because I used a wheelchair, she said modeling school would only boost my self-esteem—not lead to a real career.

No—I couldn't join the high school play. *No*—I wasn't admitted to broadcasting school after graduation. The reason? "No one would want to help the girl in the wheelchair."

No—You don't qualify. *No*—That's not for you. *No*—You're not good enough.

Those "NOs" became a heavy weight—shadowing every step, dimming my confidence, and whispering doubt into my spirit. They didn't just come from strangers, but from institutions, gatekeepers, and even people I trusted. Each "no" seemed to reinforce a message I never asked to carry that my Blackness, my disability, and my dreams somehow couldn't coexist.

By the time I graduated from high school, I could count on one hand the number of successful women I had seen who looked like me—Black, disabled, and ambitious. Representation felt like a rare jewel, and I was constantly searching for signs that someone like me could rise.

Yet, somewhere deep inside, I still believed there was *more* for me. That belief—fueled by faith, grit, and purpose—guided me forward. Even when doors closed, I kept living, rolling, and praying. I knew I was created for more than rejection. I was made for purpose.

This chapter is a reflection of that journey—and a few of the many ways I continue to grow and rise as a Black woman with a disability in leadership. Today, I stand not just as a wife and mother of two but also as an award-winning disability advocate, film producer, and national speaker. But more than any title, I stand firm in my worth as a child of God.

Even when society doesn't believe in me, I believe in myself—and in the God who made me. My life is no longer defined by the "NOs" I was given but by the "yes" I chose to live out loud.

The Early Days: Facing Rejection And Doubt

Growing up with a physical disability, the expectations placed on me were painfully low. People rarely asked what I *wanted* to do; instead, they told me what they thought I *could* do. Future job options were usually assumed to be basic office roles, store greeter positions, or other low-paying jobs typically associated with wheelchair users. It felt like society had already written my script—and the ending wasn't supposed to be successful. But I dared to dream differently.

I dreamed of being a lawyer, a model, an actor—or working in the media. Why not? I didn't see those dreams as far-fetched. I saw them as *possible*—because deep down, I believed I was more than the limitations others placed on me.

Today, I know people with disabilities who are lawyers, scientists, doctors, social workers, entrepreneurs, actors, and yes—models. They are thriving in boardrooms, classrooms, hospitals, and on stages. When workplaces are accessible and adaptive technology is available, the sky is the limit. We are proof that the problem was never ability—it was always *access* and *attitude*.

But it wasn't that way back then—and truthfully, it often still isn't. Unemployment remains disproportionately high for people with disabilities, especially Black disabled individuals. Biases run deep. The leadership roles, school clubs, and extracurriculars my peers had access to were rarely offered to me. Many decisions were made without me, even when they directly impacted my life.

Still, I knew I was meant for more. I've always been a fighter—by nature and by necessity. I had to be. I wasn't just fighting for visibility; I was fighting for a voice.

Looking back, I now realize my first step into leadership didn't come with a title or a position. It began with *self-advocacy*.

At 12 years old, I made a bold move that changed the course of my life. It wasn't a grand moment to the outside world—but for me, it was **powerful**. It was the moment I stopped waiting for someone to speak up *for* me and decided to speak up *for* myself. That single decision lit a fire in me—and that fire has been guiding me ever since.

A Turning Point In Sixth Grade

The pivotal shift came in sixth grade, when I decided I wanted to be in mainstream classes full-time.

Here's some context: in my school district, any child with a physical disability or a severe health condition was labeled POHI—Physically or Otherwise Health Impaired. That label determined almost everything about your education. From kindergarten through sixth grade, I was "mainstreamed" for half the day and placed in a special-education classroom for the other half.

I was grateful for the support, yet I couldn't ignore a growing restlessness. I wanted more. I wanted to learn alongside my peers from the morning bell to the final dismissal. I wanted the same homework, the same expectations, and the same chance to raise my hand in class.

So, I advocated for myself. I asked my general-education teacher what steps I needed to take, completed the required testing, and—after some tense meetings—successfully transitioned into full-time mainstream classes. It was my first big victory against a system that expected less of me.

Finding My Voice

Shortly after, my English teacher announced the annual school speech contest. Inspired by one of my greatest heroes, Dr. Martin Luther King Jr.,

I wrote a speech about equality—carefully crafting each line to reflect both his dream and my own.

When contest day arrived, my heart pounded, but my voice was clear. I won the opportunity to represent my school and went on to place second in the citywide competition. Sitting on that stage, I realized my words had power—and so did my presence.

A Ripple Effect

Looking back, I see that my push for full inclusion created ripples far beyond my own schedule. After I moved into mainstream classes, more students labeled POHI began advocating for inclusion into their district. Teachers who once assumed "separate was best" started re-examining their practices. Parents of younger students began asking new questions.

Among all the students in my special-education peer group who were older than me, I was the only one who eventually earned a bachelor's degree. That outcome wasn't about intelligence or effort; it was about *access*. Special-education classrooms often taught material several grade levels below the student's actual grade. Many of my peers struggled later—not because of their disabilities, but because of an inadequate education that left them underprepared for college.

The Mindset Of Leadership

So yes, the second step in my leadership journey was a mindset that *refused to accept limitations.* My willingness to self-advocate opened doors, clarified my purpose, and reminded me that real change began with a single decision to speak up.

When you've started from the bottom—when you've had to fight for every opportunity—you learn never to take anything for granted. The hard truth is that everyone is not treated equally, especially when you live with a disability and come from a family without wealth or resources. But those challenges also forge resilience; they teach you to see obstacles as invitations to lead. And that is exactly what I set out to do.

Finding And Building Community

In high school, my peers quickly recognized my tenacity and inner strength. As the only Black girl with a physical disability in mainstream classes, I was anything but invisible. Teachers often praised my work ethic; classmates admired how I navigated crowded hallways with confidence. That reputation helped me win the votes to represent the 11th grade on the student council—a milestone that proved leadership had more to do with determination than with walking.

Yet even with the accolades and friendships, I wrestled privately with low self-esteem. The boys I liked never returned my feelings; I assumed my wheelchair was the reason. I laughed off the disappointment in public, but inside, I feared I might always be seen as "just a friend."

Redirection After Graduation

Fast-forward to graduation. When broadcasting school denied my admission the rejection stung. For a moment, I considered shelving my media dreams altogether. Then I reframed that *"no"* into redirection. Even though a side note, that act was discrimination and against the law. If I would've known the law like I do know, I would've been right to sue. Nevertheless, a local community college welcomed me into its radio and theater programs—and in that accepting space, I discovered my purpose, my passion, and my people.

Between ages eighteen and twenty-one, life started to blossom. I drove my brand-new accessible van across campus, feeling the thrill of independence every time the ramp lowered. I joined and led student clubs, hosted two campus radio shows, acted in plays, and even wrote a one-act production of my own. Deep friendships formed over late-night rehearsals and early-morning breakfasts, and I experienced love for the first time—proof that someone could see beyond my chair to my heart.

Finding A Larger Stage

Then I discovered the Ms. Wheelchair America program. For the first time, I met accomplished, articulate women wheelchair users whose ambition matched mine. I entered the state pageant as the youngest contestant—wide-eyed, determined, and admittedly under-experienced. Although I didn't win, I stayed connected to the organization, sensing it could shape my future.

When both the newly crowned state winner and her first runner-up were unable to fulfill their duties, the director called me. Would I represent Michigan as Ms. Wheelchair MI 2006? I accepted with pride and a touch of disbelief—another reminder that persistence keeps doors open even when the first answer is "no."

At the national competition, I arrived armed with a well-honed speech and an open heart, ready to learn from everyone I met. I didn't take home the national crown, but I returned with something far more valuable: mentors, friends, and a diverse community—disabled and nondisabled—who truly believed in my potential.

The Lesson In Every "No"

From that season onward, I began to see each *"no"* as a possible pivot toward a better path. The *"YESes"* that followed—student-council victories, radio shows, state titles—became milestones marking for how far I'd come and hinting at how far I could still go. They affirmed that I was capable of far more than the world had ever expected of me—and, more importantly, far more than I had sometimes expected of myself.

Every redirection, every unexpected opportunity, whispered the same truth: my story was never meant to fit inside anyone else's narrow expectations. I was rewriting the script—one bold decision, one fresh chapter, and one hard-won "yes" at a time.

Building Community, Finding Courage

With my newfound community surrounding me like a protective embrace, I discovered something I had never possessed before—the courage to take risks. This support system became the foundation that allowed me to step boldly into one of the biggest leadership opportunities of my life: starting a 501(c)(3) nonprofit organization called Women Empowered Inc.

The vision for Women Empowered was born from my own experiences and the stark reality I witnessed daily. We founded the organization with a clear mission—to support and uplift women with disabilities, helping them live their best, most independent lives possible. Rather than simply offering sympathy or surface-level assistance, we focused on something transformative: *entrepreneurship*. We believed that by offering comprehensive classes and personalized mentorship, we could help these remarkable women launch their own businesses and achieve true financial independence.

I was incredibly proud when we secured our first major grant, along with office space at the prestigious Rehabilitation Institute of Michigan in Detroit. Walking into that office for the first time, knowing that we had created something real and meaningful, felt like a victory - not just for me, but for every woman who had been told she couldn't achieve her dreams.

One of our greatest and most fulfilling successes was our *comprehensive entrepreneurship program*. We watched with pride as around fifteen determined individuals went through our series of intensive workshops, each one growing in confidence and business acumen. From this exceptional group, we selected two outstanding participants who demonstrated not only business potential but also the passion and drive necessary for success. These women received seed money to launch their businesses, and witnessing their transformation from idea to execution was nothing short of inspiring.

Another moment that remains etched in my heart happened during the holiday season. We decided to surprise a disabled mother of two with Christmas gifts for her family. It was a relatively small act in the grand scheme of things, but it reminded us powerfully of the ripple effects of community and compassion. The joy on her face, the tears in her eyes, and the gratitude in her voice reinforced why we had started this work in the first place.

At just twenty-two years old, I was—as I still am today—deeply passionate about advocating for women with disabilities. My own lived experience, combined with the sobering statistics I had studied, made it crystal clear: women with disabilities face multiple, intersecting barriers. We don't just navigate the challenges of disability; we also confront systemic inequality based on race, gender, and socioeconomic status. These barriers don't exist in isolation—they compound and amplify each other, creating obstacles that can seem insurmountable.

When I first started the organization, I'll be honest—I didn't know much about the practical aspects of running a nonprofit. The paperwork, the grant applications, the board meetings, the financial management—it all felt overwhelming at times. But I was incredibly fortunate to be surrounded by wise, supportive mentors who guided me along the way with patience and wisdom. These remarkable individuals helped me grow into leadership, showing me through their example that with clear vision and strong community, truly anything is possible.

Eventually, life circumstances led me to make the difficult decision to close the organization as I began the journey of building my family.

Although that particular chapter came to an end, it had laid a strong, unshakeable foundation for my continued growth as a leader and changemaker. The lessons learned, the relationships built, and the confidence gained would carry forward into every future endeavor.

One of the most valuable and enduring lessons I learned during this time is that *authentic leadership* isn't about being the smartest person in the room. Instead, it's about having *a clear, compelling vision*—and surrounding yourself with people who not only share that vision but who are willing to roll up their sleeves and work together to bring it to life.

Overcoming Fear: The Faith Factor

After the whirlwind of graduating from college, getting married, and having children back-to-back, I made the practical but difficult decision to stay home and step away from full-time work. Like so many families across America, we found ourselves caught in an impossible middle ground— childcare costs were astronomical, and while my husband earned just enough to disqualify us from most assistance programs, his income wasn't sufficient to comfortably cover childcare, monthly bills, and all the other expenses that come with raising a family. The math simply didn't work in our favor, so I remained at home until our children were old enough to attend preschool and kindergarten.

When the timing finally felt right, I eagerly returned to the nonprofit world, first by volunteering with Warriors on Wheels, an organization close to my heart, and later by working with AmeriCorps through Public Allies/Healthy Dearborn. A little later, I received a full-time employment opportunity at Michigan Disability Rights Coalition to lead a program first for parents of color with children with disabilities and then facilitate a leadership program for non-profit organizations. I led that program at Michigan Disability Rights Coalition until unexpectedly July 16th, 2025, I will share more later in this chapter, the lesson I learned. These experiences reignited my passion for community service and reminded me of the profound impact that dedicated individuals can have on their communities.

But on the media side, there was still a dream burning bright inside me. A dream that had never dimmed despite years of being told it was impossible. I wanted to do exactly what the broadcasting school I had attended a decade earlier told me I couldn't do: produce films that mattered, films that told stories that needed to be told.

Back then, Michigan's film industry was experiencing a renaissance, thriving due to generous state film incentives that were attracting productions from around the country. I saw this as a golden opportunity and decided to step out on faith, determined to prove every single naysayer wrong. That leap of faith led me to produce my very first documentary, a deeply personal project called "My Girl Story."

At the time, I had accumulated a few small film credits through various projects, but I had never produced a full-length film from start to finish. The scope of the project was daunting, the challenges numerous, but I was absolutely determined to tell the story I wished someone had told when I was younger—the complex, nuanced story of Black girlhood, especially when viewed through the lens of disability. I drew inspiration from my own journey, filled with its highs and lows, and from my sister's experiences as part of Generation Z, watching her and her peers navigate a world that often tries to silence or systematically overlook young Black women.

I reached out to a trusted filmmaker friend, someone whose artistic vision I deeply respected, and asked her to direct the documentary. Together, we embarked on the challenging but rewarding process of finding the right subjects for our film. Eventually, we connected with two incredible young Black women—one of whom had a disability—who courageously entrusted us with their most personal girlhood stories. Their vulnerability and honesty became the heart of our documentary.

The project took ten long years and consumed much of my own money—savings I had carefully accumulated, credit cards I maxed out, and countless sacrifices along the way. There were moments when I questioned whether I would ever see it completed, moments when the financial strain felt overwhelming, and moments when the technical challenges seemed impossible to overcome. But we persevered, and we did it.

After the film was finally completed—a moment that felt like giving birth to a long-gestated dream—we organized community screenings and post-film talkbacks. These events became some of the most meaningful experiences of my career, as we heard directly from audience members whose lives were touched, challenged, or transformed by the stories we had chosen to tell. "My Girl Story" was incredibly well-received by critics and audiences alike, and I'm proud to say it's now available on major streaming platforms, including Amazon Prime and Tubi, reaching audiences I never could have imagined when I first conceived the project.

This success represents another powerful example of transforming a crushing "no" into a resounding, triumphant "yes."

The lesson I want to share is this: if you truly believe in yourself—and in the dream that God has placed in your heart—you absolutely must keep going, even when the path seems impossible. One of the most important lessons I've learned as a leader is this fundamental truth: to move forward in life, you must find the courage to overcome fear and hold tight to what I call *the faith factor*.

When the No Comes Unexpectedly

Leadership, for me, has never been about titles or praise. It's been about building, guiding, and doing the work even when the path is unclear. But I've learned—especially as a Black disabled woman—that sometimes, even when you follow all the rules, the *no* can come unexpectedly. Here is the story and the lesson I learned from working at Michigan Disability Rights

Coalition (MDRC).

For the last seven years, I've been working at MDRC. The non-profit prides itself on building community for the disabled community and creating lasting change. I believe in these values and over the last three years, I have been leading a program with heart, strategy, and accountability. I collaborated closely with my supervisor, meeting regularly to align on the curriculum, timelines, and speaker lineup. When challenges came up, I spoke with the supervisor. I communicated my concerns, asked for support, and followed the leadership advice I was given. I didn't sit back—I *led*.

However, in preparation for the work, I was ready at the beginning of our last meeting July 16, 2025, to confirm details with my supervisor. Instead, at the meeting, I was blindsided and was let go from the organization without any recourse or say.

Suddenly, the very things I had delivered were now used to question my capability. I was told I hadn't done enough—even though the milestones had been clearly defined, approved, and met. No one paused to ask, clarify, or support before decisions were made. Just like that—I was gone.

The final reason given was "team restructuring."

But the truth is, sometimes, leadership can become uncharted. Sometimes, office politics or the lack of communication or miscommunication can lead to wrongful dismissal.

But here's what I know now: Their "No" does not cancel my "Yes." The *no* can come unexpectedly.

However, their dismissal wasn't the end of my leadership—it was a recalibration. That experience taught me that as a leader, life happens, but when one chapter ends, another chapter begins. I feel it in my spirit and bones that I have been released to do what God intends me to do in this season. I'm grateful for the time I spent there and all of the people I've met.

I left this job not defeated—but affirmed. My voice matters. My leadership is valid. And my purpose isn't based on my employment but just a vehicle to use to create change.

Living A Life Of Yes

My life today is a living reflection of a powerful, transformative shift—from hearing "no" at every single turn to discovering the incredible beauty and possibility that comes with "yes." If we travel back to the very beginning of my story, you'll see that my journey is living proof that even a life initially shaped by constant rejection can transform into one overflowing with possibilities, purpose, and joy.

Growing up as a chocolate-brown African American girl who used a wheelchair, I often felt like I was caught in a relentless storm of rejection. The word "no" seemed to echo around me constantly, becoming the soundtrack of my childhood and adolescence in ways that were both heartbreaking and, ultimately, character-building.

They said *no*—the boys I developed crushes on in junior high and high school never liked me back. I watched from the sidelines as they chose other girls, always wondering what was wrong with me, always questioning my worth. And when one finally did show interest in ninth grade, my heart soared with the kind of innocent joy that only a teenager can feel. But that joy was crushed when he later admitted, with the casual cruelty that only adolescents can muster, that he had only dated me because he felt sorry for me. The reason? You guessed it—because of my disability. That revelation cut deeper than any physical pain I had ever experienced.

But now, as a proud, confident chocolate-brown, Black woman who has learned to love herself completely, I've found my resounding *yes*—in love, in life, and most importantly, in myself. I first had to embark on the challenging but essential journey of finding my own worth and value. Once I discovered that treasure within myself, I was finally ready to fall deeply in love with the man who would become my husband, my partner, and my greatest supporter.

They said *no*—I couldn't be a model. Even though a modeling agent once looked at me with what seemed like genuine interest and told me I had "a great look" and was "really cute," she still delivered the devastating blow. Because I used a wheelchair, she explained, modeling school would only serve to boost my self-esteem—it would never, ever lead to a real career in the industry. The subtext was clear: no one would want to see someone like me representing their brand.

But then I found my *yes*—not just once, but twice, when I had the opportunity to model in a statewide disability awareness campaign. Standing in front of those cameras, wearing beautiful clothes and knowing that my image would help change perceptions about disability, felt like the sweetest form of vindication.

They said *no*—I couldn't participate in the high school play. The drama teacher barely looked at me during auditions, and I knew before the cast list was posted that my name wouldn't be on it. The rejection stung, but it didn't kill my love for performance and storytelling.

But years later, I found my *yes* when I performed in theater and wrote a one-act play at my community college. Sitting on that stage, delivering lines, feeling the audience's engagement with my words—it was everything I had dreamed of and more.

They said *no*—I wasn't accepted into broadcasting school after graduation. The reason they gave me was particularly cutting: "No one would want to help the girl in the wheelchair." They painted a picture of me as a burden, someone who would require special accommodations and slow down everyone else's learning.

But I found my *yes*—not just in one project but in producing six different film projects and currently developing another that promises to be my most ambitious yet. Each project has been a middle finger to everyone who said I didn't belong in this industry.

They said *no*—you don't qualify. They said *no*—that's not for you. They said *no*—you're not good enough.

But I found my *yes*, again and again: *Yes*, I was qualified to participate in prestigious national fellowships that have shaped my career trajectory. *Yes*, I was worthy of being mentored by brilliant, successful people like comedian W. Kamau Bell and television executive Ashley McFarlin, both of whom saw potential in me when others saw only limitations. *Yes*, I was capable of leading complex nonprofit programs that made real differences in people's lives. *Yes*, there are programs and opportunities specifically designed for someone exactly like me. *Yes*, I am more than good enough—I am **exceptional**.

Still, I want to be completely honest: somewhere deep inside, even during my darkest moments of rejection, I always maintained a flickering belief that there was more for me. That belief—fueled by unwavering faith, determined grit, and a clear sense of purpose—guided me step by step from a life dominated by "no" into a future filled with unlimited "yes."

Now, I won't pretend that life still doesn't come with its share of hardships and challenges. The "NOs" still sting when they come, and they do still come. Fear still shows up uninvited at my door, sometimes when I least expect it. *Imposter syndrome* is painfully real and can make me question everything I've accomplished. All of these feelings are completely valid, and they remain part of my ongoing journey.

But this chapter of my life is a reflection of how I continue to show up and grow as a Black woman with a disability in leadership positions. I stand firmly in my worth as a beloved child of God. Even when society doesn't believe in me, even when systems try to exclude me, even when individuals underestimate me, I believe wholeheartedly in myself—and in the God who created me with intention and purpose.

I've accomplished goals that I once thought were completely out of reach—building a meaningful, impactful career that allows me to make a difference, nurturing deep, authentic relationships with people who see and value me, and serving my community in ways that create lasting change.

Saying *yes* means being courageously open to new experiences, even when they scare me. It means embracing challenges as opportunities for growth rather than obstacles to avoid. It means trusting the process, even when I can't see the entire path ahead. Most importantly, it means understanding that failure or being told *no* isn't the end of my story—it's simply a lesson on the winding road to discovering and fulfilling my purpose.

My journey from "no" to "yes" continues every single day, and I'm excited to see where it leads next.

About the Author

On July 2nd, 1985, at just six months old, Tameka Citchen-Spruce was involved in a horrific car accident that left her paralyzed from mid-chest down. Growing up as a young Black woman with a physical disability hasn't been easy, especially when it came to learning to love herself. However, based on her life experiences, Tameka developed a deep passion for disability advocacy and media.

Her journey began at 21 years old when she was crowned Ms. Wheelchair Michigan 2006, using her platform to speak out about supporting women with disabilities who are survivors of abuse. Just two years later, she founded Women Empower Inc., with the mission of empowering women with disabilities to live their best lives.

Tameka went on to study Broadcast Television and earned her bachelor's degree in Journalism from Oakland University. With a unique blend of journalism and activism, she learned the power of storytelling and the importance of lifting up voices that are too often silenced.

Her award-winning short film, *Justifiable Homicide*, and her documentary, *My Girl Story*, which has been selected for several film festivals, are examples of her commitment to telling powerful, untold stories.

She served as the Co-Director of LEAD, a leadership development program for BIPOC disabled individuals and their parents at the Michigan Disability Rights Coalition. She also volunteers with Warriors on Wheels of Metro Detroit, focusing on criminal justice reform for people with disabilities.

Tameka has been selected for esteemed fellowships including AmeriCorps, Public Allies of Metro Detroit, and the Detroit Equity Action

Lab at Judge Damon Keith's Wayne State University Law Center. She was also honored to serve as a Disability Delegate at the Congressional Black Caucus Legislative Conference and is a proud member of the National Black Disability Coalition.

Both professionally and personally, Tameka recognizes the deep connection between race, gender, and disability. She has read the statistics, heard the stories, and lived through the systemic barriers that affect her community. Through her work, she aims to advocate, educate, and elevate media representation of the BIPOC and disability communities in ways that are unapologetic, engaging, and thought-provoking.

One of the most important roles in Tameka's life is being a wife and mother of two children—a role that continues to shape and inspire everything she does.

How to Connect with Tameka:

LinkedIn: Tameka Citchen-Spruce

Facebook: @Tameka Citchen-Spruce

Instagram: @Divas In the City Digital Series

Acknowledgements

I want to first thank God and my Lord and Savior, Jesus Christ—without Him, I can do nothing. I'm also deeply grateful to my family, especially my husband, children, parents, sister, and brother. I truly appreciate all the love from my in-laws, cousins, great-uncles, aunts, and grandparents—three of whom are now ancestors, and one who is still with us on this side of heaven. And last but certainly not least, thank you to my best friend, close friends, mentors, and the beautiful community I'm blessed to be a part of. I'm here because of all of you!

Dr. Yulanda Harris, Ed.D, CNP

Trailblazer in Neurodiversity Leadership
Visionary CEO & Advocate
Distinguished Scholar & Practitioner
Influential Speaker & Educator

Introduction: My Unconventional Path to Purpose

My leadership journey was not easy as a neurodivergent Black woman. *Removing the Mask and Finding My True Self in a Neurotypical World* is more poetic and personal, focusing on the liberation that comes from no longer masking. I did not have a clear, straight-line path to success. And throughout my career, it felt like a revolving door of different roles, industries, and experiences. In fact, it was a puzzle with pieces that did not seem to fit. For decades, I was what some might call a "job hopper," moving from one position to the next. Despite many successes, I was driven by a restless and unshakeable feeling that whatever role I landed, it was not my true calling. It was not until I was diagnosed with Asperger's Syndrome (autism spectrum disorder) at the age of 58 that the pieces finally fell into place. I realized that everything that was going on inside my brain was, in fact, my greatest strength. You see, my journey was not a series of *"She can't keep a job."* In fact, it is a masterclass in adaptability, resilience, and cultivating a career on my own terms and God's plan and purpose for me.

I have finally come to terms that my late-in-life diagnosis was not a defeat but *a revelation*. And now, I am allowed to reframe my entire professional history. Guess what? All those different jobs, the moments of uncertainty, the continuous search for something more, weren't signs of being lost. They were seasons of learning, growing, and building a foundation that was uniquely my own. I discovered a profound truth: working all of those jobs was not as bad as I thought they were. Lessons learned. Could I have done things differently or taken a more diplomatic approach? Absolutely. It created a path of something greater where I cultivated my career and leadership style, more importantly, learned from each and every encounter, lacking executive functioning skills; however, sometimes, creating a persona (Masking) that showed me how to navigate the complexities of my leadership journey.

This book is a testament to that journey—a tribute to all of my neurodivergent colleagues, and a call to action for every woman who feels their journey is unconventional like mine. It is a powerful opportunity to share my voice, to inspire others with my leadership journey, and to be part of a collective movement of impactful women. I want this story to resonate with anyone who has ever felt out of step with the world, to show that your unique path is your greatest asset. With this understanding, I embrace my story, own my journey, and display how I dared to dream in leadership and in life.

Removing the Mask: Finding My True Self In A Neurotypical World

Life Before My Diagnosis

My life before my diagnosis was a constant, exhausting performance. For as long as I can remember, and even now, I navigate through a world where I do not fit in, you know that awkwardness and not understanding unwritten rules, a language I still do not consider to be good at. I am a Black woman, a natural leader, and an advocate, but on the inside, I am always struggling to belong. I am too nice, too direct, too emotional, too naïve or clueless, too "something," and unfortunately that just doesn't fit. And now, I realize the Asperger's or autism spectrum disorder (ASD) diagnosis is not a curse; it is, in fact, *a blessing*. It is the key that finally unlocked the mystery of my own existence, revealing that my perceived flaws are simply a part of how my brain is wired.

From childhood through adulthood, the feeling of being an outsider was a constant companion. I literally struggled. I was a people pleaser; a shield I used to deflect the confusion and anxiety that came from not knowing how to act. And unfortunately, I felt forced to please, leaving me vulnerable, and I was often taken advantage of, both personally and professionally. I was always searching for a place to belong, a community where I could be myself without the constant fear of saying or doing the wrong thing.

I do believe that this search for a constant need to feel appreciated and valued led to that pattern of "job hopping," as I moved from one company to the next, convinced that the next workplace would finally be the one where I fit in. Same in my personal life involving friendships and relationships. The emotional toll was enormous. It was the overwhelming weight of loneliness, the exhaustion of constantly trying to be someone I was not, and the deep-seated belief that I was fundamentally broken.

The professional world, in particular, was a trial of challenges. As a Black woman with what is now understood as high-functioning autism, my directness and intense focus on ethics were often misinterpreted. While I saw myself as an advocate, my employers saw me as difficult or insubordinate. My inability to engage in small talk or social interactions was seen as standoffish. The need for clear, direct communication, which is a characteristic of my neurotype, often clashed with corporate cultures that valued subtleness and hierarchy in the workplace. My professional life is a combination of complex achievements and advocacy. I am a visionary and a natural leader in my own right, driven by a strong sense of ethics and a desire to do what is right - that often has me at odds with practically everyone I encounter. And can you believe that my career spans over 35 years in Human Resources?

Challenges Along the Way

One vivid memory stands out from the 1980s. In the dead of winter, I showed up to work in a pantsuit. At the time, an unwritten dress code dictated that women only wear dresses or skirts. And here it is, my simple act of choosing comfort and practicality over an unwritten rule was perceived as an act of defiance. I was not being insubordinate because for me, it was a matter of common sense. Yet, this simple choice became my first act of defiance and an indication of the laundry list of professional challenges to come.

My refusal to conform, to sacrifice my comfort for an arbitrary standard, was seen as a lack of respect for authority. This pattern repeated itself throughout my career, my integrity and directness were often perceived as aggression or a lack of team spirit. I was not insubordinate; I was just being myself. And for a neurodivergent Black woman in a neurotypical world, that was often a radical act.

Family Life

From a young age, I was different to my family, especially to my siblings. Even though they were overprotective of me, and still to this day, they did not understand me or had very little patience with me during the times of me advocating for myself. They saw my differences, they felt them, but remember, during the 60's and 70's, there was no name for it. "We always knew you were different," my one sister stated. And another sister thought I was being a "drama queen," a label I now understand was her attempt to make sense of my emotional outbursts, my stims, my meltdowns, and more importantly, my need to feel understood.

For years after my diagnosis, I tried explaining my behavior, my brain, my sensory needs, my way of processing the world. I sent articles, shared books, and talked about what it meant to be neurodivergent. Then, I realized I was trying to force my world on to them, and it was something they either chose not to understand or just couldn't. Putting in that effort was exhausting, and the results were often disheartening, leading to conflicts and contentious conversations that resulted in distance. I will take responsibility for some of the distancing because I did not know how to regulate my emotions at times.

I have come to recognize that their understanding may remain limited, despite the deep bond we share—a value instilled by our mother, who emphasized the importance of family. This does not reflect a personal shortcoming, nor does it indicate any absence of affection on their part. And it is simply the reality of our different paths in life.

Today, I have found a beautiful peace in this acceptance. I do not need to force my family to understand me. I love them, and our connection exists regardless of their understanding of my inner world. You see, my journey to acceptance was not just a personal one; it was also a reflection of a larger cultural narrative within the Black community. In the 1960s and 70s, terms like "Aspergers," "autism," or "neurodivergence" was non-existent. My community was fighting for our very existence, and the focus was on external threats. There was little space to discuss the complexities of our internal worlds. What was "different" was completely misunderstood or often looked at as some type of mental illness where I would hear older family members saying things like *"something's wrong with them?"*

As child and now an adult who struggles with eye contact or have repetitive movements, I was often seen as "shy" or "odd." My need for routine and my unique way of communicating could be seen as a character flaw rather than a different operating system. There was a prevailing stigma that compared any deviation from the norm to a mental illness, and mental illness was not something people talked about. We were taught to be "strong," you had to "push through," and you do not talk about family personal business. As a result, this *cultural silence* left many of us with no name for our experiences, no community to lean on, and no understanding of our own unique strengths.

So, in the end, the protective love from my siblings was their way of caring for something they did not have a name for. But in the space of that silence, many individuals like myself, we created our own world, found our own languages, and learned to love the way our minds work. We are now breaking that silence, giving a name to what was once left unsaid, and paving the way for a future where all Black minds are celebrated for their differences, not condemned for them.

Academic Achievements

I started my doctorate in Educational Leadership mainly to prove my worth. I needed to show not only myself but everyone who had ever doubted me, every subtle look of dismissal, every stereotype I'd fought against. I needed to show myself that I was more than what they saw. A doctorate felt like the ultimate validation, a shield that stems from hard work and sacrifice that would protect me from the world's judgment.

I often felt like I was operating on a different wavelength than everyone else. Even though it did not seem like it on the surface, I was exceptionally observant. I had a deep-seated need for structure and routine, and I found immense comfort in immersing myself in subjects that captivated my interest. But in a world that often values conformity, my unique way of being is often misinterpreted. It was not until I received my diagnosis of Aspergers (autism spectrum disorder) as an adult that I finally had the language to understand myself and my brain.

My journey through academia was initially a quest for validation. I decided to pursue a Doctorate in Educational Leadership, not just out of a love for learning, but because I felt a desperate need to prove my worth to my family, to my peers, and most importantly, to myself. I believed that earning the highest degree would finally silence the voice of self-doubt that hung over my head for years, and now, I realize that my drive for learning is a fundamental part of who I am.

The knowledge I gained was not just a collection of facts; it is a set of tools for navigating the world I live and exist in. My education gave me a framework for understanding not just my own experiences but the experiences of countless others. My doctorate did not just give me a title; it gave me the confidence and the intellectual tools to advocate for myself and my community.

Today, as a leader, I continue to carry the lessons of my academic journey with me. I have learned that leadership is not about fitting a mold; it's about leveraging your unique strengths and creating spaces where others can do the same. My neurodivergence, once a source of insecurity, is now **my superpower**. It allows me to approach problems with a fresh perspective, to find patterns and connections others might miss, and to lead with a deep sense of empathy and authenticity. Yesssss! My doctorate gave me the courage to step into my power and to lead, not in spite of my neurodivergence, but because of it!

I finally embrace my neurodivergence. My ability to hyper-focus allowed me to uncover connections and patterns that others might have missed. My unique perspective, shaped by my identity as an African American woman with Aspergers, offers a different lens through which to view educational systems and leadership. I am not just proving my worth; I am creating it.

When I finally held that diploma, it was not the relief I had expected. It was a quiet sense of triumph. The true reward was not the piece of paper; it was the person I had become. The doctorate gave me the intellectual tools and the confidence to navigate the world on my own terms and the path that God is leading me. It taught me that my drive for learning is a core part of who I am, and it is a gift that no one can ever take away. I no longer feel the need to prove myself. Now, I am free to learn, to lead, and to simply be *me*.

The Turning Point

They say life is a journey, and for a long time, mine felt more like a maze with no map. I always knew I was different, but I couldn't put my finger on why. It was a constant, depressing thoughts of *"what's wrong with me?"* that followed me everywhere. For years, I was a woman on a quest to be fixed or healed, sitting in therapy offices and being given a different story every time.

They called it anxiety, depression, and maybe even a personality disorder. It was not until 2018, at the age of 58, that the puzzle pieces finally clicked into place. I am a Black woman diagnosed with Aspergers or autism spectrum disorder (ASD). And even though the diagnosis was a shock, it explained a lot. All those times I felt like I was being true to myself, it took such an emotional toll, often leaving me praying that I would go to sleep and never waking up because the mental toll was too much; and all this time, I never knew that my nervous system was on fire from overstimulation, triggers, and anxiety that I did not have the tools to manage or cope. Remember, I was a product of the '60s and '70s, and back then, it was not heard of in the black community. And for me it was a silent struggle, a battle fought behind closed doors. I couldn't talk about it because I did not know what it was, so I was left to figure it out on my own.

And now my diagnosis has been the key that unlocked my healing journey. It was a long, hard road of reflection, confronting my past self, and a lot of tears. I had to face the ways I was misunderstood, the bridges I'd burned, all because I did not have the tools resources, language or understanding to explain what was going on. There's a certain pain that comes with realizing you've been misunderstood for so long and that you've misunderstood yourself just as deeply. I had to grieve the person I was and the life I could have had if I'd known sooner. But I can't live there anymore that is full of regrets and mistakes all because I was not aware.

And now, I have made peace with my past. The bridges I burned are lessons learned. I have come to understand that my "different" is not "wrong." It is just a different way of experiencing the world, a unique perspective that I am finally learning to embrace. My journey has been messy and difficult, but it is mine. And I wouldn't trade it for anything, because it led me to be the leader and visionary I am today. A woman who is finally, truly, and unapologetically herself, all because God created a brain in me that is so unique and different for me and the world to embrace.

2018: The Year of Diagnosis

For nearly six decades, I existed in a world that never quite made sense. I was misunderstood, an outlier, and a woman carrying a burden of silent struggles that I couldn't even name. That all changed in 2018, at the age of 58. I was in therapy, trying to make sense of my past mistakes I made in life and why I just couldn't let go, when my therapist said something that would fundamentally alter my reality. He suggested that my symptoms sounded a lot like what was then called Asperger's Syndrome.

It was a moment that my life forever changed and how I realized that I had to start over because I *masked* for so long. Because how could I be an undiagnosed neurodivergent person at almost 60 years old? And then came a series of "ah-ha!" moments. The social awkwardness; the overstimulation that cause my triggers and mood swings; the deep, intense passion for always wanting to create something new and unique; coming up with creative ideas in the workplace that was considered too ahead of the game or they were not prepared to move so fast with what I presented; and the way my mind always seemed to be running on a different operating system than everyone else's.

It was at *that* moment how my experiences aligned with the diagnostic criteria was a moment of reflective clarity. With this new understanding, I began the slow, intentional work of my healing journey. I weaned off the medications that were masking my true self and replaced it with practical strategies and tools (**DO NOT ATTEMPT TO TRY THIS ON YOUR OWN WITHOUT MEDICAL ADVICE**). Please know that my way *does not* work for everyone, because without having these medications, it can lead to a psychotic episode. This way of managing and coping takes daily practices to help me manage my unique way of processing the world. I am still learning and growing every single day, becoming a better version of myself, not by changing who I am, but by understanding and embracing the woman I was always meant to be. This diagnosis was not an end; it is a beginning. A fresh start to live a life built on self-compassion and authenticity through the Grace of God!

Processing the News

My entire life has felt like a puzzle with a missing piece. I was always the "different" one, the one who did not quite fit in, and no one, not even me, could figure out why. I was a Black girl just trying to survive in a world that was not built for me, and on top of that, I was neurodivergent. But I did not know that then. All I knew was that I *felt* like I was living on a different planet than everyone else.

Funny story. I remember when I went to get help and I told the psychologist that I did not belong here. He said, "Where, on this earth?" And then, it happened. My diagnosis. And a long road that led me to where I am today. I can still remember the feeling of these emotions hitting me all at once—relief, confusion, and anger because I was not "normal."

The relief was the first thing I felt. It was a deep, soul-shaking sigh that I'd been holding in for decades. I finally had an answer. The puzzle was not missing a piece; it just had a different shape. This was not a flaw in my character or some type of mental illness. I was not broken. I was just different. That single truth was the beginning of my healing journey. It was the moment I started to give myself the grace and love I had been so desperately seeking my entire life.

But right behind that relief came the confusion. I had to re-examine my entire life, every memory, every experience, every misunderstanding, through this new lens. All those times I was told I was "too much" or "not enough," all those moments I was labeled "sensitive" or "dramatic," all those years I spent exhausted from trying to mask who I was. It all made sense now, but that understanding brought a wave of questions. *Who was I, really, underneath all the masking and pretending? And how was I supposed to build a new life with this knowledge?*

The confusion quickly morphed into anger. I was angry for all the wasted years. All the energy I spent trying to be someone I was not. All the pain I endured from being misunderstood. I was angry at a world that did not know how to *see* me. I was angry at myself for not knowing sooner. I experienced strong anger that I needed to acknowledge and reflect on before moving forward. It was necessary to allow myself time to process those feelings.

Once I had processed those initial feelings, I knew I had to tell people. It was a terrifying decision. *What if they didn't believe me? What if they didn't understand? What if they saw me differently?* But sharing my diagnosis with my family and close friends was an essential step for my healing. It was a risk, but it was a necessary one. I couldn't continue this journey alone. I deserved to be *seen*, to be *understood*, to be *loved* for exactly who I am. And I deserved to move forward with a full heart, surrounded by the people who truly love me.

Recognizing the Signs

The path to truly knowing myself hasn't been easy, but it has been the most liberating journey of my life. For as long as I can remember, I felt like I was speaking a different language than everyone else, always a step behind, always trying to fit a square peg into a round hole. My whole life felt like one long misunderstanding.

My healing began the moment I started to see myself not as a broken version of normal, but as **a masterpiece** in my own right. It started with me recognizing the signs of autism in my own life. I consumed books, articles, and every online community I could find. I was desperate to understand what was going on with me.

I finally had names for the things that had always bewildered me— *sensory processing, executive functioning*, and the *social dynamics* that felt like a secret club I was never invited to. And then, I learned to painfully unmask. Because I masked for so long, I did not know who I was. In an instant, I had to do away with *the mask* that I had been wearing my whole life to please others. When I finally allowed my *authentic* self to shine, I began to thrive. The most valuable tools on my journey have been understanding my own triggers, learning to set boundaries without guilt, and finding my voice. This new understanding has ignited a fire in me, a passion for advocating for other neurodivergent individuals, especially in the workplace. We deserve to be seen, heard, and celebrated for exactly who we are.

Tools for Understanding

This may sound like a broken record but for my whole life, people tried to give me a name, but they just couldn't find the right one. They said I was "too much" or "not enough." Too sensitive, too direct, not social enough. They'd call me "difficult" and "weird," and for the longest time, I believed their lies. I spent so many years trying to fit into a mold that was never made for me, and all it did was leave me cracked and broken.

But when I finally got my diagnosis, it was like the world suddenly made sense. It was not a flaw; it was a map to my own mind called **neurodivergent**. With that map in my hands, everything changed. I started to see my so-called "challenges" not as weaknesses but as my very own superpowers. My intense focus? That's what makes me a strategic leader. My need for structure? That's what allows me to build solid, reliable systems. My blunt honesty? It is the foundation of trust with my team.

Today, I am a leader who is not just thriving but I am blooming. I am building a world where people like me aren't just tolerated, we're celebrated. I am mentoring other neurodivergent professionals, helping them find their voice and own their power. My relationships, both at work and at home, are the realest they have ever been because I am finally showing up as my authentic self. This is not just a career; it is *a calling*. And it is a testament to what happens when you stop running from who you are and start loving every single part of it.

And my most valuable tools? A better understanding of my own triggers, learning to set boundaries, and discovering a passion for advocating for neurodivergent individuals in the workplace.

Life After Diagnosis

My whole life, I was a puzzle piece from another box, trying to force myself into a picture that was never mine. I was always misunderstood, always feeling like I was "too much" or "not enough." I was that little Black girl who did not fit in, who was always a little bit off. People did not get my intensity, or my way of seeing the world in patterns and details that they missed. I carried that weight, that quiet shame, for so long.

Then, the diagnosis came. And in that moment, I was not a broken person that needed to be fixed; I have finally given myself permission to let go of a lifetime of shame. It was the moment I finally got to say, *"Oh, so this is why,"* and started my journey toward healing. The whispers of "she's nice, but there's something about her that's not right," turned into a powerful understanding of how my brain works. The loneliness I felt was replaced with the realization that my brokenness in the world's eyes was just me being "Autistically Beautiful." I was just different. Besides, did you know that there is beauty in broken pieces?

Now, I am here. A leader. A founder. A visionary. I built the NeuroDiversity Inclusion Institute because I had to create a space I never had. We are out here advocating for people who are just like me, helping them turn their struggles into strengths. And with Trainingphase, we are showing companies how to open their doors and their minds to the vast talent neurodivergent people bring to the table. I have taken the very things that made me feel like an outsider and used them to build a community where no one has to feel that way.

I used to see all my unique traits as obstacles, but they are not. They are my superpowers. My different way of seeing the world is not a flaw; it is *a gift*. It helps me to lead with a fierce kind of authenticity and mentor others who are still finding their way. I am no longer trying to shrink myself to fit into a box that was never meant for me.

My relationships, my joy, my whole life—it is all more real, more vibrant, because I am finally embracing the beautiful, complex Black woman I am. I am thriving, not in spite of my neurodivergence, but because of it. My journey is proof that being different is not a flaw, but a superpower, and my hope is that others can find that same sense of freedom and belonging.

Closing Reflections

If you're out there and this resonates with you, I want to speak from the deepest part of my soul. For as long as I can remember, I felt like a puzzle piece that did not fit anywhere—not in my family, not in school, and definitely not in the professional world. I was the Black girl who was "too much" and "not enough" all at once. Too loud when my passion was on full blast and too quiet when the world around me was overstimulating. I was the one who could see the patterns in everything but somehow missed the social cues and sarcasm that everyone else seemed to understand instinctively. My whole life was spent being misunderstood, and honestly, that misunderstanding felt like a weight I was destined to carry forever.

My whole life I thought I was a problem that had to be solved. They would say I was too emotional or that I needed to be more "personable." I spent so many years trying to force myself into boxes that were never meant for me, and I was so tired. But here is the thing that I have learned: *your life is not a mistake.* It is a masterpiece in the making, and you, my sister, are the artist. For me, the first step on my healing journey was finally getting that diagnosis. It was not a label to shrink me down; it was a map to guide me back to myself. It was the moment I realized my life was not a glitch in the system; it is a feature. God made me this way on purpose.

Your truth is waiting for you to find it. Do not be afraid to pull on the loose threads of your own story. Ask the hard questions. *Why do I feel this way? What do I need to do to thrive?* Dig for those answers, even if They are buried under years of people telling you who you should be. You have to be brave enough to embrace your authentic self, with all its beautiful complexities. That's where the real power is—not in trying to conform, but in living in your truth.

This journey can feel lonely sometimes. I have had so many nights where I felt like the last person on Earth. But I want to tell you something: you are not alone. There is a whole community of us, a beautiful, diverse and brilliant neurodivergent minds. Our unique perspectives are not a burden; they are a gift to the world. We are the problem solvers, the dreamers, the ones who see the world from a different angle and find solutions others can't.

This journey of healing has been a testament to God's love and grace in my life. He has carried me through every moment of misunderstanding, and every night I spent in tears feeling alone. The power of prayer is what has sustained me. My daily scripture readings remind me that I am enough as I am and bring me peace. So, hold your head up high. Your journey is valid, your voice matters, and your existence is a testament to the beautiful, expansive nature of humanity and God's perfect design.

About the Author

Dr. Yulanda Harris is a force for change in the world of neurodiversity. Driven by a deep passion for unlocking the unique talents and perspectives of neurodivergent individuals, she champions their inclusion in all aspects of life. Her unwavering dedication manifests in a multifaceted career encompassing leadership, advocacy, education, and action. As CEO of Trainingphase Consulting Group, Dr. Harris empowers organizations to embrace Neuroinclusion, fostering workplaces where neurodivergent individuals thrive. This expertise extends beyond the corporate sphere, with her role as CEO and Advocacy & Mediation Representative for the NeuroDiversity Inclusion Institute (NDi) further amplifying her impact. NDi is a testament to her commitment to championing equal opportunities and resources for the neurodivergent community.

Dr. Harris's leadership stems from a rich tapestry of experience. Over 35 years in human resources and talent management, including leadership as Chief Organizational Development Officer, equipped her with a nuanced understanding of organizational dynamics. Her academic foundation is equally impressive, boasting a Doctorate in Educational Leadership and Management, a Master's in Human Resource Management, and a Neurodiversity Professional certification. This expertise is further honed through her active participation in the Stakeholder Engagement Group for PCORI and the University of Pittsburgh's research team on mental health outcomes in neurodivergent adults. In addition, Dr. Harris is the original founding & honorary co-advisor for the Neurodivergent Student Alliance at Oakland Community College creating a footprint to start the organization.

Dr. Harris is not one to let knowledge gather dust. She inspires action, translating her expertise into impactful presentations, workshops, and interviews that disseminate knowledge and foster inclusive dialogue. She has authored professional articles and curricula, shaped understanding, and built resources for the neurodivergent community. Her dedication goes beyond words. She founded NDi Institute, a dedicated organization empowering individuals and advocating for systemic change.

Dr. Harris is more than a speaker; she is a bridge builder. Her unique blend of expertise, lived experience, and unwavering dedication make her a powerful voice for neurodiversity. She ignites conversations about embracing differences, unlocking potential, and building a future where everyone's contributions are valued and celebrated. Dr. Yulanda Harris is not just a champion for Neuroinclusion; she embodies progress.

How to Connect with Dr. Yulanda Harris Ed.D, CNP:

LinkedIn: Yulanda Harris, Ed.D, CNP

Facebook: @chapmanforever

Instagram: @ndiinclusion

Acknowledgements

This book is a love letter to my mother, my first and greatest teacher. A single mom who built a fortress of love and security around me. She taught me what it means to be a strong, compassionate, and authentic Black woman. Mama, you showed me how to live in my truth, and this work is a testament to the foundation you laid. I feel your absence every day.

To my father, though we were estranged, I still want to honor you. My journey of unmasking is also a journey of understanding the past, and I hope this book can be a path toward healing.

To my son, this book is a direct result of your love and understanding. You're the only one who ever truly saw me, the woman behind the mask I wore for a neurotypical world. You did not ask me to change; you just looked at me and said, "It is okay, Mom." That simple phrase changed everything. Your love gave me the courage to embrace who I am, and your support gave me the strength to tell my story. Thank you for making it all okay.

To my siblings, this journey has been a long one, and you've been a part of it from the very beginning. I know this book might bring up a lot of questions, and maybe some of it feels foreign or even a little strange. That's okay. What I hope you do understand, though, is that this is me. The *real* me. The person I have always been, underneath the performances and the attempts to be "normal." Your support, even when you did not quite know what you were supporting, has been a foundation for me. You are my home, my first audience, and my greatest cheerleaders. Thank you for loving me, even the parts you can't see yet.

I want to extend my deepest gratitude to my pastor, Reverend Dr. B. Kevin Smalls and the entire community at HOPE United Methodist Church. For so long, I felt like I had to wear a mask just to exist, especially in spaces where I was not sure if my true self would be understood or embraced. But at HOPE, I found a sanctuary—a place where the mask could finally come off. Your unwavering acceptance, Reverend Smalls, has made all the difference in my journey. You helped create a truly safe space for me and so many others, reminding me that my neurodivergence is not something to be hidden, but a beautiful part of who I am. The love and support I have received from this church community have been a beacon of light, guiding me as I learned to unmask and find my voice. I am forever thankful for the grace and understanding that you have all shown me.

To my friends, colleagues, and chosen family, you came into my life during different seasons—some for a while, others for the long haul. And for that, I am forever grateful. You've held space for me, without judgment, in a world that was not built for a brain like mine. You saw me when I was still wearing the mask, and you were there when I finally took it off. You witnessed the stumbles, the stutters, and the moments of profound breakthrough. This journey has been a long road, but it is one I never had to walk alone.

Thank you for seeing me in my fullness, for loving me through the mess, and for reminding me that it is okay to *just be.* My hope is that this book helps others find their own peace, their own freedom, and their own truth—and in doing so, know that they are more than enough, just as they are.

Dr. Karwanna D. Irving

Multi–7-Figure Business Owner
Ranked #21 on the SF Business Times Top 100 Fastest Growing Private
Companies in the San Francisco Bay Area
Named to the 2025 Inc. 5000 List of Fastest-Growing Companies in
America
2025 Enterprising Women Award Recipient
Featured in Success Magazine (2023) as One of the Most Influential
Women in Business

From Food Stamps to Fortune: The Dr. Karwanna D. Irving Story

Born to Lead: The Early Signs

When it comes to leadership, resiliency, and overcoming adversity, there's a lot I can share. I am Dr. Karwanna D. Irving. Today, I am known as a first-generation multimillionaire, a wealth creator, a coach and mentor, a mother, and a recognized leader in business and finance—but it wasn't always that way.

Leadership is one of those qualities you either have or you don't. Skills can be developed and improved, but if you weren't born to lead, it eventually shows. For me, I've always believed I was born to lead. As far back as I can remember, I stood out by being good at many different things—abilities that naturally set me apart from my peers.

When I was in kindergarten, my brother's teacher often called on me to help him with his math homework. He was four years older than I was, yet I already knew multiplication tables that stumped kids twice my age. His teacher would shake her head in amazement, wondering how such a young girl could grasp concepts that challenged much older students.

Another one of my older brothers often got into trouble at school. His teacher would call me out of class and hand me a note to deliver to my mom. She trusted me to do the right thing, even though I knew it meant my brother would end up getting a whooping when we got home.

Yep, I said whooping and not spanking, because being Black and having a Black mama, that's exactly what you got when you acted up around grown folks. Those teachers saw something in me that I couldn't see in myself at the time. Looking back now, I understand what they recognized—it was my trustworthiness. Even as a child, I was reliable and responsible. Those are the very qualities that shape a natural leader.

Southern Roots, California Dreams

I was born the fourth of seven children to a single mother who migrated from Louisiana to San Francisco, California, in the mid-1970s. That period was part of the Great Migration from the South—a time when many Black families left behind oppression in search of opportunity in the North and West. They came to work in shipyards and warehouses and to buy real estate at prices that now seem unimaginable. My mother carried the weight of seven children on her shoulders as she chased the promise of a better life.

I was only two when we arrived. Aside from faint memories of horses and cattle on the farm my dad once had, I don't recall much about back home. Still, fragments of wide-open spaces and the smell of fresh earth would return in my dreams, quiet reminders of a simpler time before the challenges of city life took hold. I often say I'm a native California girl with Southern roots—the best of both worlds, though I wouldn't fully appreciate that heritage until much later.

Growing up was tough—especially being in the so-called "working middle class," which was really just another way of saying "poor-like." We weren't dirt poor like the homeless people we'd see on the streets, but we lived in almost every low-income housing project in the city and got those welfare cheese boxes. Looking back now, I know we were only a couple of paychecks away from hitting rock bottom. And that was even with my mom in school to become an RN while running a side hustle doing jheri curls at the kitchen table.

My mother was a warrior disguised as a gentle woman. She'd come home from nursing school, exhausted from long hours of studying anatomy and pharmacology, only to set up her makeshift salon in our tiny kitchen. The smell of chemical relaxers and the sound of sizzling hot combs filled our apartment as my mom transformed the hair—and the confidence—of women in our neighborhood. She was my first example of a true entrepreneur, balancing textbooks and hair products with the determination of someone who knew survival required multiple streams of income. At the time, I didn't have a name for what she was doing.

I remember being in middle school and asking my mom for lunch money. Instead of handing me cash, she gave me a book of food stamps. The shame I felt in that moment was overwhelming. I can still picture the way the other kids stared when I pulled out those colorful coupons instead of crisp dollar bills. That was the moment I told myself I would do something bigger and better when I grew up. It lit a fire in me—a determination to never feel that kind of financial vulnerability again.

Finding Faith in the Foundation

Since my mom always kept us in church, I learned early how to pray for the things I wanted. The church became my refuge—a place where I could dream beyond my circumstances. By the time I was eleven, I was so deeply involved that I kept going even when no one else in my family did. Eventually, I convinced my younger brother to join me. While other kids my age were sleeping in on Sunday mornings or finding excuses to skip service, I was drawn to the sanctuary like a magnet.

Church was where I built resilience, faith, and determination—the very qualities that would one day help me achieve what most only dream about, though that fulfillment wouldn't come until decades later. The sermons about overcoming obstacles, the gospel songs about breakthrough, and the testimonies of triumph over adversity planted powerful seeds in my young mind. I absorbed every word, every lesson, every promise that God had something greater waiting for those who stayed faithful through the storm.

The church ladies often commented on my maturity and the way I carried myself with wisdom beyond my years. After service, they would pull me aside and tell me that God had His hand on my life, that I was destined for something special. At the time, I thought they were just being kind, but their words became prophetic reminders that echoed in my mind during my darkest moments.

The American Dream Deception

I loved the 1990s. It was the greatest era in hip-hop, my high school years, and the time when I transitioned from childhood to early adulthood. The music spoke to my soul—artists like Tupac, Biggie, and Lauryn Hill painted vivid pictures of struggle and triumph that resonated with my own life. During that season, I embraced the ideology of the "American Dream": go to school, get a job, buy a house, get married with the white picket fence, and live like the Joneses until retirement. I was determined to make that vision mine.

I thought I had it all figured out. I became the first in my family to walk across the stage and earn a high school diploma, the first to attend college and obtain a Bachelor of Arts degree, and the first to secure a well-paying job earning $80,000–$90,000 a year by the age of twenty-two. The pride on my mother's face when I graduated was worth every late night of studying and every sacrifice we had made as a family. I wasn't yet married with the picket fence, but I did have a daughter and a bunch of bills I had to keep up with. And I was never able to land a job in my field of education —and that's when I realized the so-called "American Dream" was really a system designed to keep you programmed. You give all your time in exchange for money that barely covers the basics.

I often wondered how people managed to work full-time while raising children. By the time you drop them at daycare, head to work, return to pick them up, get home, and cook dinner, you're left with only two or three hours together before it's time to sleep and start the cycle again. The rat race was relentless, and I felt trapped in a routine that resembled survival more than living.

As determined as I was to change the narrative by becoming rich and wealthy, I quickly learned that the rat race I had bought into wasn't going to take me there. The math didn't add up—no matter how hard I worked or how many hours I put in, I was always just getting by, never moving ahead. I ended up in the very situation I had sworn to escape living in low-income housing, relying on food stamps, and barely making it.

The irony was crushing. Here I was—college-educated, professionally employed—and still struggling to make ends meet. The American Dream had turned into the American Nightmare, and I felt like I was drowning in financial mediocrity.

The Awakening: Breaking Free from the Matrix

And then I said enough was enough. I took my life into my own hands, stepped out on faith, and made a firm decision: I would become part of the country's top six percent of revenue earners. The choice came suddenly but with absolute clarity—like a switch flipping in my mind. I refused to accept that this was as good as it gets.

When I began researching the wealthiest people in the country, I discovered that nearly all of them were entrepreneurs. Very few had followed the illusion of the American Dream. In fact, many had dropped out of school early, and some didn't even hold a high school diploma. The statistics were staggering. Names like Bill Gates, Steve Jobs, and Richard Branson—college dropouts who had rejected the traditional path and built success on their own terms—shattered everything I thought I knew.

So much so that I decided to leave my traditional 9-to-5 and start my journey toward millions at the young age of twenty-seven—and I never looked back. The day I walked into my supervisor's office to hand in my resignation was both terrifying and exhilarating. I was walking away from the security of a steady paycheck, health insurance, and possibly some retirement benefits to chase a dream most people would have called crazy.

I had a little money saved when I set out on my entrepreneurial path, but my credit was ruined, I had no blueprint, and not a single person I could turn to for guidance on where to begin. What I did have was an unshakable conviction that one day I would become the first in my family to make millions. That belief outweighed my fear, drowned out my doubts, and carried me through obstacles that would have stopped me otherwise.

The School of Hard Knocks

The crazy thing about starting your own business is that if you don't have a blueprint, you'll end up scattered—working hard but going nowhere. The only knowledge I had come from common marketplace myths: "It's going to take three to five years to build a business," "Don't expect a profit until year five," and "You're lucky if you make it to five years, and you must bootstrap your way to the top." To me, that meant the only way forward was to become a relentless go-getter who refused to quit.

Mary Kay Cosmetics was the first MLM business I joined, investing just $500 to get started. I didn't wear makeup, and I definitely didn't make it far with that venture, but I walked away with lessons that shaped my foundation. I learned the importance of building a business where God comes first, family second, and everything else after. That philosophy of faith, family, and career aligned deeply with my values—even if the pink Cadillac dream never came true.

I also learned that success required more than just hustle—it demanded a complete shift in mindset. That's when I discovered great thought leaders like Zig Ziglar, Jack Canfield, Napoleon Hill, and many others who seemed to hold the secret to lasting success. At first, it felt almost magical. The more I listened to their words, the more my perspective changed, and soon my thoughts began shaping my reality. They say the mind is a terrible thing to waste, and I found that to be absolutely true.

Their teachings opened my eyes to the power of positive thinking, setting clear goals, and the law of attraction. I consumed everything I could—books, audio programs, seminars. These mentors became my virtual coaches, guiding me as I shifted from an employee mindset to an entrepreneurial one.

Fast forward from Mary Kay Cosmetics to Dyson Fashion Plus—a company I started selling church dresses and accessories to first ladies and evangelists—then to Big Mouth Productions and finally She's Got Goals, LLC. That decade was the making of Dr. Karwanna D. Irving. Each business became a steppingstone, a lesson in disguise, equipping me with skills I didn't realize I would need for the journey ahead.

It's amazing how something small can grow into something far greater than you ever imagined. But the only way to find out is to withstand the fire, the trials, and the tribulations without giving up. I'm reminded of a scripture I used to hear sung in the church choir when I was young, from Ecclesiastes 9:11: "The race is not given to the swift, but to the strong that endureth until the end." Back then, those scriptures didn't mean much to me, but today they've become guiding principles—truths that continue to shape both my personal and professional life.

As I was building in the midst of divorce, repossession, depression, and the obstacles so many face in life, I stayed determined to see my millionaire dreams come to fruition. The divorce was especially devastating—not only emotionally but financially. Legal fees, divided assets, and the stress of starting over while trying to build a business nearly broke me. There were nights when I questioned everything, when giving up seemed like the only logical option.

But because I've always been the type to share what I learn as I'm learning it, my struggles naturally became my ministry. Growing up in adversity had humbled me and shaped a heart to serve and love God's people. I knew that the freedom and success of many others depended on my willingness to succeed first, so quitting was never an option. In that way, my business became my ministry.

The Breakthrough: Discovering the Trillion Dollar Secret

Five years into business, I was barely making $30,000 a year. That's enough to make anyone want to go back to a regular job—at least then I would have benefits and a retirement plan. The thought crossed my mind more than once. The security of a steady paycheck looked tempting compared to the uncertainty of entrepreneurship.

Still, even with that temptation, I couldn't bring myself to walk away. I had already invested too many years, too many sacrifices, to simply give up. That resilience eventually led me to discover what I came to call the Trillion Dollar Secret to Government Contracts. At the time, I had no idea that I could do business with the government—or that they were obligated to do business with people like me.

A billionaire friend I had met shared the secret with me, and that's when everything clicked. He explained how the government was required by law to award a percentage of contracts to small businesses, minority-owned businesses, and women-owned enterprises.

It made everything I had learned about the so-called two-to-five-year business curve feel like a complete lie. I began to see that much of what we had been told simply wasn't true. There were strategies that millionaires and billionaires knew—insider knowledge that kept them in a class all on their own. The world of government contracting felt like a hidden society, one most people had no idea even existed, even though the government is the single largest customer in the world.

Once I discovered that, I committed myself—and anyone willing to follow me—to a journey toward millions. I threw myself into learning everything I could: the regulations, the bidding process, the certification requirements, and, most importantly, how to position myself and my business to win contracts that could change everything.

By my mid-thirties, I was earning multiple six figures. The shift was incredible—from barely scraping by to securing six-figure contracts with government agencies. In my early forties, I crossed into multiple millions and even generated a million dollars in a single business day. That moment will always stay with me—the day when years of struggle, sacrifice, and persistence came full circle and rewarded me in ways that surpassed even my boldest dreams.

What I came to realize through it all was that the so-called "American Dream" is really just the default for people who don't create a dream of their own. Building wealth, I learned, wasn't mystical—it was about understanding the numbers and creating an action plan that allowed those numbers to become reality.

The Power of Programming and Reprogramming

There were many lessons I learned on my journey to millions, but the one that stands out most is this: there is nothing a person can't accomplish if they truly set their mind to it. The challenge is that most people are influenced by what I call programming—from a broken education system, television, media, and now social platforms. All of this noise fills their lives with negativity, shaping their belief systems, which then guide their thoughts, actions, decisions, and ultimately their ability to create wealth.

The truth is that many people don't even know who they really are. They know their names, but they don't recognize the power that lies within them. Because of that, they accept limiting beliefs—like thinking "I can't afford it." But in reality, that phrase doesn't mean it's impossible; it simply means what they want isn't important enough for them to figure out how to make it happen. I used to think that way too when I was broke. Today, I know different: you can afford anything you dream of, no matter the cost, if you are willing to be resourceful.

People often say things like "I don't have time," but the truth is, we all have the same twenty-four hours in a day as the rich and wealthy. The difference is that wealthy people use money as a tool to buy their time back. Meanwhile, poor people—or the so-called working middle class—spend a great deal of their time trying to save a little money. What they haven't yet realized is that the real value of money is its ability to create more time. And when you use money to buy back your time, you create the space for even more money to flow in.

I don't have enough space in this short book to share everything I've learned about success and leadership. But I can leave you with a principle that changed my life. It's the principle that helped me become not only a first-generation multimillionaire in my family, but also a coach and expert who has guided more than 6,000 business owners nationwide. Many of them have broken the family pattern of being "just over broke," and some have even gone on to earn millions for the first time in their history.

Over the past two years alone, my mentees have collectively generated more than $31 million in revenue through government contracts. That impact is what led to my being featured in Success Magazine, named a 2023 Influential Woman in Business, and ranked #21 on the San Francisco Business Times list of the Top 100 Fastest Growing Companies in the Bay Area, and ranking #1680 in Inc. 5000 2025 Fastest Growing Private Companies in America I've also been recognized as a leader on ABC, CBS, List TV, and other major media outlets—and was honored with the United States Presidential Lifetime Achievement Award.

The Be, Do, Have Success Principle

And that principle is what I call the Be, Do, Have Success Principle. To achieve any result in life—whether in love, relationships, finances, or anything else—you must first become the kind of person who is willing to do what it takes to get there. This is the great secret that some of the most influential thought leaders in history—Zig Ziglar, Jack Canfield, Napoleon Hill, and others—have pointed to. It is also laid out in the book of Genesis, which provides the foundation of passion, purpose, and prosperity.

In the beginning, God created the heavens and the earth. "God" here represents identity. He established who He was before He began to create. That is the Being in Be, Do, Have. After establishing His identity, He began the work: dividing darkness from light, separating the waters from the land, creating fish, birds, and every living creature, and commanding them to reproduce after their kind. That was five days of doing and delegating—the Doing in Be, Do, Have.

And on the sixth day, God did something remarkable. He partnered with other creators, and together they made man in His image. Notice how the doing took more time than the being. Then came man's first commandment, found in Genesis 1:28: "Be fruitful and multiply, replenish the earth, and subdue it"—all instructions for doing. And only then comes the promise: "and you will "have" dominion."

The truth is, God had already laid it all out for us, but the message often got lost because church messengers didn't fully see it as a practical principle for abundant living. Even the word subdue carries great meaning—it speaks of overcoming, prevailing, and rising above. In other words, God had already equipped us with what we needed to endure and conquer the challenges that would arise in the process of doing.

Even God faced disruption. When darkness covered the earth and His intention was to create, He overcame it by declaring, "Let there be light." That moment shows us that even He confronted obstacles—and solved them. In the same way, He knew we would face disruptions and would need to know how to respond when they came. Yet many people mistakenly view disruption as a sign to give up and start over. The truth I've learned is different: disruption is not the end, but the moment to endure and press forward. My prayer is that this understanding strengthens you on your own journey—both to succeed and to endure, no matter what comes your way.

Breaking the Chains of Mental Slavery

Matthew 9:35 reminds us that the harvest is plentiful, but the laborers are few. In the same way, there are countless opportunities available to anyone who truly desires to change their life and the direction of their family's future. I know this is possible. The truth, however, is that most people never act on these opportunities because of a hidden set of rules and systems designed to hold them back. I'm no longer blind to these influences. These invisible programming systems shape what you believe about yourself and the world. They show up in the education system, in cultural expectations, and in the traditions and values we inherit.

Every day, we are bombarded with subtle messages that distort our perspective. They convince you that anything capable of transforming your life must be a scam, while at the same time presenting the very scams that keep you broke, struggling, and excluded from opportunities as if they were reality.

When I was trapped in that programmed system—and even now, as I continue working my way out—I can look back and identify the beliefs that kept me living beneath my potential. I didn't care about credit, because I had no idea what leveraging other people's money could make possible. I believed debt was always bad, shaped by commercials that preached getting out of debt as the only way to achieve "financial freedom."

I also avoided the idea of a mortgage. To me, it felt safer to stay in low-income housing than to take on what I thought was unnecessary risk. What I didn't realize was that owning real estate, especially rental properties, is one of the most common assets the wealthy use to create passive income—the kind that allows them to stop trading time for money and build lasting freedom.

Even the holiday system had me scrambling to find money—New Year's in January, Valentine's Day in February, Spring Break in March, Easter in April, Mother's Day in May, and the list went on. I didn't see it at the time, but all of this was programming me—and everyone else—to be consumers instead of investors.

Now that I've broken free from that cycle, I see it clearly. And today, I feel blessed to be a vessel of truth and light, showing others how to free both their minds and their money so they can live more prosperous and abundant lives.

The Harvest is Ready

But the truth is, not everyone is ready to break free from their programming. All I can do is share the message, and those willing to put in the work to change their lives will reap the harvest.

To date, I've helped more than 6,000 business owners position themselves to work with the world's largest client—the U.S. government. A number of them, together, have generated over $31 million in additional revenue. That growth gave them the financial freedom to build new legacies for their families.

I don't believe money is everything, but I do know the power it brings. More money means better health options, the ability to live in thriving communities, and the freedom to choose a lifestyle instead of settling for one by default. It also allows us to pass down wealth and assets so future generations aren't forced to start from zero. This is how we begin breaking the chains of poverty in our families and communities.

This is what some of the greatest figures in history have done—families like the Vanderbilts and the Rockefellers. But you don't have to live through the success stories of others. You can create that life, and even more, for yourself. That's God's true purpose for His people. And in case you're wondering—yes, you deserve it.

My journey from food stamps to fortune is not just my personal story; it's a blueprint for anyone willing to challenge their programming, step out in faith, and put in the work to transform their life. The harvest is ready, and those willing to labor will reap abundantly.

If you'd like to learn more about how I help everyday people become first-generation millionaires, visit ContractstoMillions.com.

About the Author

Dr. Karwanna D. Irving is renowned as a Government Contracts Expert, Transformational Speaker, Author, and Business Wealth Coach. Her impactful expertise has earned international recognition, being prominently featured across major news outlets and magazines including Fox 2 News, Ticker News, The List TV, Business News Today, Median, International Trade News, Global Investing Today, Brainz Magazine, Woman to Woman Talk Magazine, The Female CEO, Influential People News, Digital Buzz, EnspireMagazine, She is E Magazine, and many more.

Her voice and insights have reached global audiences through appearances on notable podcasts such as Earn Your Leisure (EYL) Podcast and Myron Golden Podcast. Dr. Irving's collaboration extends to co-authoring a book with acclaimed speaker Les Brown, and she has graced stages alongside influential figures.

Recognized for her exceptional contributions, Dr. Irving was nominated as Success Magazine's Woman of Influence. Her authored book, "Don't," stands as a testament to her expertise and dedication to empowering entrepreneurs.

As the Founder of the fully accredited Dream Achiever College University, accredited by the Better Business Bureau, Dr. Irving has led the charge in aiding over 1,602 entrepreneurs in securing prequalification for government contracts in the last 2 years alone. Additionally, her guidance has assisted hundreds of small businesses in generating millions of dollars in revenue. The media has bestowed upon her the title of "millionaire creator," highlighting her unparalleled ability to transform aspirations into tangible success stories.

Driven by a true passion for elevating lives and turning dreams into reality, she embodies the role of a dedicated Mompreneur, wife, and executive CEO, balancing the intricate interplay between business and family life.

How to Connect with Dr. Karwanna:

LinkedIn: Dr. Karwanna Irving

Facebook: @Karwanna D. Irving

Instagram: @Karwannadspeaks

Acknowledgements

I want to first honor and thank God for the many blessings He has bestowed upon me, and for choosing me as His vessel to be a blessing and light to others.

I also want to thank all of my mentors and coaches, including Myron Golden and his brother Jeff, Joel Erway, Marquel Russell, Dr. Sonja Stribbling, Taurea Avant, and others, who have given me the tools and the confidence to break outside of my comfort zone, and become the best version of myself in every way.

I am so grateful for my children, Tylea Eison, Jevon Dyson, Markaila Dyson, and Sir Carter Irving, for being the number one reason why I do what I do, and for inspiring me to create a lasting legacy.

To my mom, who has always had my back, no matter what, through both good and bad decisions, thank you.

To my community of followers, mentees, colleagues, and teammates, your support means the world to me.

And last but not least, I want to thank my husband, who's always been my number one cheerleader and support person, someone who's willing to go to the moon and back with me.

Juliet Romeo

Screenwriter
CEO Media Jules Production at Media Jules LLC
Founder of Slamdance UNSTOPPABLE Film /Curator/Programmer

FADE IN:

Opening Scene – Crash

Fluorescent lights hum above my head. The hospital hallway smells like bleach and irony. I'm in a gown, not a power suit. Tethered to oxygen, not a mic. My phone buzzes on the tray beside me — another missed call, another missed meeting. The world outside keeps spinning, and I'm stuck in a scene that was never on the vision board.

Only hours earlier, I was moderating a high-profile Hollywood panel with two of television's most in-demand disabled actors, riding the high of visibility, creativity, and momentum. I was running on fumes, still pushing through the final touches of a production deadline. But this wasn't just the usual exhaustion. I was silently battling something far more dangerous—a blood clot had formed, and I didn't know it yet. What I thought was just me "pushing through" like always was actually my body waving a red flag. But like so many of us who lead and lift others, I didn't stop—not until the crash came.

This isn't what leadership looks like. Not according to the books. Not according to the panels, the podcasts, or the LinkedIn quotes. But this? This is where I found it.

Not in the boardroom. Not in a title. In the stillness of a hospital room, where breathing is a luxury and faith becomes non-negotiable. In the silence between pain and purpose.

In the choice to keep showing up — for myself, for my calling — even when my body had every reason to opt out. Because *real leadership* doesn't always enter with applause. Sometimes, it crawls in quiet. Sometimes, it sits in a waiting room and prays it will be seen.

Sometimes, it learns to lead from a bed you didn't choose, in a body that's been through hell, holding on to a vision too big to quit. They don't tell you that *power* can sound like a whisper. That survival is *strategy*. That *purpose* doesn't pause for pain.

But I know it now. Because I lived it. And I'm still here.

CUT TO BLACK

Unscripted: A Life in Motion

FADE IN:

Scene One – Hidden Figures

You know the scene in *Hidden Figures* when Dorothy Vaughan walks into that IBM room, takes one look at the machine nobody knows how to run, and decides she's going to learn it anyway? Nobody invited her in. Nobody trained her. Nobody believed she had the skills. But she taught herself and then turned right around and brought her entire squad with her. That's the kind of energy I've lived my whole life with.

Before I was anyone's "director," "founder," or "trailblazer," I was the girl in the hospital bed. Again. Missing another school trip. Missing another class presentation, I had worked too hard on. Missing out. Doctors came and went like scene changes. My classmates kept moving forward while I pressed pause on my life — one blood transfusion, one oxygen tank, one "I'm sorry, she can't participate" at a time. I wasn't the student council type. I wasn't the athlete. I was "the sick girl." Quiet. Fragile. Strong, but somehow always fading. I was diagnosed with sickle cell disease at six months old before I even knew how to talk. I knew how to express pain. A shared trait from both of my parents but neither of them could really understand what I was going through. I felt like no one did. I learned perseverance at a young age.

When I was three years old, I remember overhearing a doctor telling my mother that I would never get out of this hospital bed and that I would never sit up on my own. I was confused because I knew that I could walk. I could sit up like a big girl, I could do a lot of things. *What was this man talking about?* I'd been trying to sit up and it was hard, so I just gave up and laid back down. I tried again and there was so much pain. I just laid back down, but I remember opening my eyes every day and the first thing I did was try to sit up. I did that every day until one morning, that doubtful doctor walked into the room and he saw me sitting up eating some Jell-O, and I looked at him and pointed my spoon at him when I said, "See, I told you I knew how to sit up." I always say the best way to convince me to do something is to tell me that I cannot do it. That personal challenge - or what some might call *stubbornness* - kept me going. But it is a gift and a curse sometimes.

"You're so strong. I'm proud of you for being so smart. I can't believe how smart you are."

Well, yeah. I had nothing but time to read books and use my imagination. When your body is locked down, your mind becomes the escape hatch. They didn't tell me I was developing marketable skills. They didn't tell me I was practicing creative control, world-building storytelling. They just told me I was too sick to do anything.

They told my mother I wouldn't live to see 25, maybe not even 15. So even with all the hope and pride she carried for me, I can only imagine how terrifying it was to dream, to believe in more for a child the world had already counted out.

Thank God I had a praying mother. A praying grandmother. That's why I'm still here. But I get it now. How hard it must've been for them to raise me with hope in one hand and statistics in the other. How impossible it must've felt to place bold expectations on a little girl everyone believed would never physically amount to anything.

And when you add the weight of systemic bias, the way healthcare underestimates Black and Brown bodies, and the way society withholds investment until we've over-proven ourselves, it becomes a recipe for quiet hopelessness.

While other kids were outside making snow angels or splashing in sprinklers, I was indoors learning to direct my dolls, creating characters out of action figures, writing short stories where my best friends had powers and the girl like me was the main character. I built whole worlds from a twin-sized hospital bed and a window that barely opened.

What they didn't see, and what I didn't see yet, was that I was becoming a leader in silence. A director in disguise. A girl who would one day turn all that isolation into impact.

I didn't know then that being left out would teach me how to make room. That being the misfit would one day be my creative superpower.

I wasn't a figure in anyone's plan. I was *hidden*. But I was *never* lost.

SMASH CUT TO:

FADE IN:

Scene Two – The Book of Eli

I didn't just learn to lean on my faith in waiting rooms or in the stillness between test results. I called on my Lord and Savior, Jesus Christ, with every breath. That kind of faith wasn't new to me. It was poured into me from birth.

I was raised by a praying mother and a praying grandmother. I saw what it looked like when Black women went to spiritual war. I watched my grandmother go into full-on prayer warrior stance, like it was weaponry, like it was the only thing standing between me and an early obituary. I watched my mother lay hands on my body while doctors shrugged their shoulders. Their faith held me up until mine could stand on its own.

But I didn't just mimic their words. I learned faith for myself. I wrestled with doubt, with depression, and with self-destruction. Because I always felt like there was more. I just didn't know how to access it.

I knew I wasn't built for an ordinary life. Even as a child, I felt it in my body, something *deeper* was calling me. But no one was saying, *"You're going to be great."* They were saying, *"You're too sick."* They were telling my mother, *"She might not make it to 15."*

So even with all the love and pride my mom had for me, I can imagine how scary it was for her to dream big dreams on my behalf. To believe in me more when the world and the system kept expecting less. They didn't want to place the weight of unrealistic expectations on a child they were told would never physically amount to anything. And when you combine that with the healthcare bias Black families face? It's a recipe for hopelessness.

Still, something inside me kept pushing. But without direction, that push turned into pain and then into confusion. I didn't know how to harness the fire. So, I rebelled. I stumbled. I doubted. I broke things, including myself.

Until one night, in the hospital, my body felt like it was being burned from the inside out. Every inch of me was in pain. It was so bad, I begged God. Literally begged Him to cut off my legs. *"Take them, Lord. Just take the pain with them."* That's how bad it was.

And when I finally made it through that crisis, I felt guilty. Guilty for wanting to get rid of the very limbs God gave me. Guilty for being so desperate that I asked Him to erase a part of me. But then came *the shift.*

The next time. And of course, with sickle cell, there is always a next time. That next pain crisis, when my body felt like a world war on the inside. Instead of begging, I started praising. I was still in pain, still shaking, still weeping, but I changed the words.

I started saying, *"Thank You, Jesus."*

"Thank You, Lord."

"Thank You for breath."

"Thank You for being with me, even now."

I praised Him right there in the pain. And it confused the nurses. One said, *"What is she even thanking Him for?"* But the head nurse, a woman who felt the Spirit in the room, shut it down.

She said, *"Don't disturb the Holy Ghost in here."* And I'll never forget that.

That night, God reminded me that I wasn't broken. I was built different. *Gratitude* became my superpower. Not because it erased my pain, but because it gave me power in spite of it.

That's when I truly understood my faith. It wasn't just a thing I inherited. It became my weapon.

My compass. My source.

And that's when I knew my leadership didn't have to look like anyone else's. It didn't need a platform. It didn't need permission. It needed obedience. I wasn't chasing titles. I was answering an assignment. My story didn't start with applause. It started with scripture scribbled in margins, with tears soaked into pillows, with deep exhales in sterile hallways, and God's whisper saying, *"Keep going, my child."*

No, I never had it all together. But I knew exactly *who* was holding me together.

FADE TO LIGHT.

FADE IN:

Scene Three - The Devil Wears Power Suits

(Performing Leadership, Losing Self)

I never wore a power suit. That was never my vibe. I've always been that girl—moving to the rhythm of my own beat: offbeat, loud, vibrant, different. If everybody loved something, you could bet I didn't. I'd fall head-over-heels for a bomb outfit in a store window until I saw someone else wearing it. That's all it took. It was already done. Played out. I wanted to stand out, not blend in.

Before purple hair was trending, it was mine. A signature. Bright. Bold. Unapologetic. The kind of hair that made people stare. Some snickered. Some whispered. Some even copied. I wore it anyway. Because one thing about me? You're not going to forget me. You couldn't, not with a name like Juliet Romeo. My grandmother made sure of that. She wasn't even in the delivery room when I was born, but she made my mother promise not to name me until she arrived. For two weeks, I was just *the baby.* Then she walked in, took one look at me, and declared: "Her name is Juliet." And when people realized my last name was Romeo, they swore it had to be a joke. It wasn't. It was *divine* drama. And I've been living up to it ever since.

Still, there were moments I tried to dim. Not because I didn't want to be seen—but because being seen as disabled, as sick, felt like too much. *Internalized ableism* is slick. It doesn't yell. It whispers. It tells you your access needs are inconveniences. That your cane, your oxygen, your accommodations make you less—less beautiful, less capable, less worthy. It took me years to realize I wasn't hiding out of humility. I was hiding out of shame.

I tried to run the academic race like everyone else. But sickle cell doesn't care about semesters. I had to stop and start, drop out, return, withdraw, and repeat—just to survive. While my peers walked across stages, I was relearning how to walk again. I was laid up in hospital beds. But I never stopped trying. My classes? Easy. The education system? Not so much. Getting sick without proper support from the disability office was brutal. I walked into offices and be told, "Well, you don't look sick. You don't look like you have a disability." Being forced to ask my doctor over and over again to prove my condition just to access basic accommodations? Draining. Discouraging. And some days, downright infuriating. Because I watched certain other students walk in—students who didn't look disabled either—and get everything handed to them.

It was something ridiculous like, "Chad gets paper cuts easily, so he gets extended time for exams," while I was juggling pneumonia, kidney infections, or recovering from a transfusion, still submitting homework to stay ahead. That was my strategy: get everything done early. I worked ahead so that when the inevitable crisis hit, I wouldn't fall behind. But there were times I got knocked out mid-semester—right in the thick of midterms—and there was no backup, no understanding, no grace. Just silence.

Still, there were a few who saw me. Who poured into me. One of them was Dr. Alvin Lewis, the Director of the Broadcasting Department, where I earned my associate degree. He saw my strength. He saw my hunger. And he didn't just cheer me on—he gave me the tools. He taught me lessons I still carry, like: "Be careful what you say and who you say it to—because you can't unring a bell." That one stuck. Especially in journalism. Because of him, I kept going.

I became a radio host. Then a journalist. Eventually, a filmmaker. I got everything I dreamed of—just not on anyone else's timeline. But even with all that success, I didn't realize how much I was still performing.

You know that scene in *The Devil Wears Prada* when Andy Sachs tosses the phone in the fountain and finally walks away from the version of success that required her to disappear? I had my own version of that. I was invited to a film festival at Google headquarters in San Francisco—major moment. My PBS documentary on sickle cell had just premiered. And now, I was about to present it live. But while sitting on the panel, I felt it: my oxygen machine was humming. Loud. Too loud. I panicked, so I turned it off.

Yes. I turned off my oxygen machine because I didn't want to make anyone uncomfortable. Meanwhile, my body was suffocating. My oximeter dropped: 90s... 82... 80... 78. I was trying to disappear in a room I had literally entered to be seen. The irony. I was there to speak about sickle cell. Yet, I was trying to hide the reality of it.

That was my breaking point. Because what was I really doing? Trading my safety for social approval? Sacrificing my well-being just to be accepted in a space that barely made space for me? I'd done it before. Wore my oxygen in the car, then took it off before class. Held my breath in interviews. Pretending that I didn't need what I clearly needed. And for what? To not be "that girl with the machine." To be seen as competent—not complicated.

But here's the truth: I *am* complicated. And competent. And chronically ill. And creative. And radiant. And worthy. And a whole lot of other things all at once. That moment at the festival taught me I wasn't a disruption. I was *a revelation.* People came up to me afterward in tears. Thanking me. Saying, "Now I see what sickle cell really looks like." They didn't see weakness. They saw a mirror. They saw a story.

So why was I still trying to wear a costume that didn't fit? It wasn't a power suit. It was a straitjacket. I had been trading my voice for approval. My authenticity for access. My rest for relevancy. All because I didn't want to be "too much." But I have been "too much" since birth—and it's exactly what makes me unforgettable.

I had to unlearn the performance. Strip off the disguise. Embrace that leadership doesn't require a costume. I lead in flats, if I need to. With oxygen, if I have to. With rest as resistance. With my faith fully visible. I'm not powerful because I perform well. I'm powerful because I live truthfully. On purpose. And from now on, I'm showing up as me. Even when it's messy. Loud. Different. Unfiltered. Because the original blueprint was never broken. It was just waiting for permission to breathe.

CUT TO BLACK

FADE IN:

Scene 4 - Everything Everywhere All at Once

(Legacy Work, Unstoppable Movement)

I never imagined that telling my story would make me a filmmaker, an advocate, and a blueprint all at once. But it did.

In the early 2000s, I met a girl named Kookie—with a K. We were both hospitalized and shared the same nurse, who kept saying, "There's another girl with sickle cell across the hall who's also from New York. You two should meet." Eventually, I made the first move. I walked across the hall and said hello. At the time, I was still living in New York, but I promised Kookie I'd call her the next time I returned to Florida. A few months later, I did come back—this time, in the process of moving to Miami—and I gave her a call. She admitted she didn't think I actually would, but she was glad I did. I'm glad I did, too, because from that moment, we became inseparable.

She helped me find my first apartment in Miami, and we made so many memories there—sharing stories, gossiping, talking about boys, relationships, and our dreams. Dreams for women like us, with sickle cell. With Kookie, I never had to over-explain. She just knew. She felt the same fears, the same pain. That kind of understanding? It's rare. We laughed through everything—our pain and our joy. We hit the clubs, did the party scene on our terms. While others pregamed with shots of liquor, Kookie and I pregamed with Smartwater, Gatorade, and doctor-prescribed oxycodone. We knew when to go home. We didn't have to push ourselves past our limits—we protected each other. Our double dates were hilariously memorable. We had a rhythm.

Then in 2014, Kookie got very ill. Sickle cell ravaged her body, and she passed away. We always talked about building a legacy for ourselves in this community. Doing something that mattered. And when she died, I felt like Kookie didn't get that chance. For the first time, I had to face my own mortality—because Kookie was me. And now, she was gone.

So, I made a decision. I took my grief and turned it into a documentary called J.U.L.E.S.—short for *Just Using Life to End Sickle Cell*. "Jules" was Kookie's nickname for me. The film was about our friendship, her family, the foundation created in her honor, and the reality of losing someone to the same disease you live with. It was my way of keeping Kookie's spirit alive. A love letter. A call to action. The film did well—better than I ever expected. It's still emotional to talk about. But it gave me purpose. And it propelled my career forward.

After Kookie passed, I didn't just grieve—I moved. The pain was unbearable, but I channeled it. I didn't know how to advocate for the sickle cell community on a large scale, so I started with the story I knew best: ours. From *J.U.L.E.S.* to *The Art of Warriors*, to speaking on panels, PBS features, and working with hospital boards and researchers—I looked up and realized I was doing everything Kookie and I had once prayed to do. Creating. Educating. Fighting. Living.

There is a moment in the film *Hidden Figures* that captures what this journey has felt like for me. It's the scene where Dorothy Vaughan—played by Octavia Spencer—delivers that iconic line: *"You know what your problem is? You don't want to know the truth. Because then, you'd have to make a change."* She was standing up—not just for herself, but for the truth. That scene lives in my bones. Like Dorothy, I found myself in rooms where people didn't expect me to belong. Rooms where they saw my condition before my credentials. My oxygen cannula before my vision. And like her, I realized that if I didn't speak the truth—if I didn't demand change—then nothing around me would change either.

Then came Slamdance. It was the middle of the 2020 pandemic, and the world was breaking open. Film festivals were going virtual. DEI statements flooded timelines. Everyone was trying to figure out how to "do better." It was messy. Imperfect. But Slamdance stayed ten toes down. They didn't just see my talent—they saw *my truth*. That's when I realized that **real leadership** *is about creating space for growth and choosing grace over ego.* Yes, there were missteps. Yes, there were gaps. But there was also trust. And from that trust, we built something. Today, *Unstoppable* is more than a program. It's a standard. It's proof that access can be intentional, bold, and joyful. It's a home for disabled creatives—not to be seen as inspiration but as an industry. Brick by brick. Step by step. With purpose.

After Kookie's passing, I became deeply focused on showing up as my full self—including being honest and upfront about my access needs. But nothing prepared me for the reality check that came during a trip to Park City, Utah, for a major film festival. Park City is one of the highest elevation cities in the United States—famous for skiing, filled with steep hills, icy sidewalks, and cold, dry air. That kind of altitude is not just uncomfortable for someone like me with sickle cell disease —it's **dangerous**. I needed supplemental oxygen, and my body was absolutely not built to thrive in that kind of environment. Still, I showed up, this time wearing my oxygen in plain view. I wasn't hiding anymore. But I was scared.

I remember standing in line in the snow, my oxygen levels dropping, wondering what would happen if I collapsed. Would anyone know what to do? Would they even know what sickle cell was? I had learned all my life that the world lacked awareness about this disease, but now it felt life-threatening. I decided to stay in lower-altitude cities like Salt Lake City and South Jordan, skipping most events. But one day, I ventured out. And *that* day changed everything.

As I stood outside in the cold, I noticed at least four or five wheelchair users trying to maneuver on the slick, icy sidewalks. It was a challenge just to stay upright. I soon found out this was the year the powerful documentary *Crip Camp* premiered. I couldn't believe it: a film about disability, by disabled creatives—yet the environment was completely inaccessible for the very community it was meant to celebrate. That was my breaking point.

I realized I couldn't wait for someone else to fix this. I needed to take what I had learned—and lived—and build something new. That's when I created a proposal for what an accessible film festival should look like. I knew I couldn't do it alone, so I got an opportunity to talk with the leadership of Slamdance, an Oscar-qualifying international film festival, also held in Utah. I asked them what accessibility and diversity look like at their festival. Their response was incredible. They listened. They understood. They saw my vision—and they invited me to bring it to life. That's how Unstoppable was born.

I chose the name because that's what we are. The disabled community is *unstoppable*. When the pandemic hit in 2020, the world came to a standstill—but we didn't. We already had been living in a remote, virtual-access world. Suddenly, everyone else was living like us. But I knew that once the world found its footing again, we'd be pushed back into the shadows if we didn't fight to stay visible. So, I fought. I advocated for closed captions, for audio description, for hybrid models of access. Unstoppable wasn't just a program. It became *a movement*. It connected brilliant disabled filmmakers and storytellers from all over the world and brought in organizations, who also had been working in isolation, tossing pebbles into the ocean. Together, we created a wave.

I've seen filmmakers come out of the Unstoppable program and go on to revolutionize how they tell stories—not just by centering disability, but by making their work *radically inclusive* for everyone. One close colleague told me that after being introduced to Unstoppable, she now builds accessibility into every script, every set, every story. That's the kind of leadership that multiplies. It wasn't just about amplifying other voices—it started with amplifying my own. As a leader, you cannot whisper when change is needed. You can't be afraid of judgment or rejection. There will be

NOs. But there will also be *YESes*. And those *YESes* will change the game. Slamdance was my yes. And Unstoppable? That is my why.

I didn't post every step on social media. I didn't always announce what I was doing. As my sister Amanda jokes, "Juliet, when did you go to Dubai and meet with the Sheikh?" We laugh. But that joke holds truth—I don't always talk about it, because I'm busy doing it.

I've worn many hats: journalist, radio host, documentarian, director, screenwriter, wife, sister, daughter, auntie, and friend. Each role is sacred. Each one deeply lived. Sometimes, it is hard to choose between ambition and personal life, but I know that everything I do is for the people I love. Even the ones I will never meet.

That moment felt like my own multiverse jump. Like Evelyn in *Everything Everywhere All at Once*, I was suddenly seeing a version of myself I hadn't dared to believe in before. A version that was already inside me, waiting for activation. One moment I was surviving in hospital beds and waiting rooms—the next, I was on stage, behind a camera, holding a mic, telling my story, and realizing it had power. I wasn't just a patient. I was an advocate.

A producer. A director. I have been underestimated, overlooked, and told I was too sick to do anything at all. And yet, I am doing *everything*. Everywhere. All at once. Because I was called to do it. Because the people I have lost—Kookie, Hertz, and others—walk with me. Because I know that what I am building is bigger than me. And because when God calls you to something—no diagnosis, no gatekeeper, no system—can stop it.

Dear God,

Thank You for trusting me with this life, this story, this body, this calling. You saw fit to give me purpose before I even had the words to name it. And through every setback, You whispered, "keep going."

So, I made a promise. I promise to lead without shrinking. To honor the body I live in, not resent it. To wear my oxygen, my purple hair, my full truth without apology. To rest without guilt and rise without fear. I promise to lead from presence not performance. To make access non-negotiable. To speak up even when my voice shakes. To speak *especially* when my voice shakes.

I promise to hold them open the doors You have opened for me. To create room for misfits disruptors and dreamers. To uplift my community without needing to be the only one seen. I thank You for the fire and the grief that shaped me. The losses that deepened my love. The rooms I have had to build because none existed before me. And still.

I do not ask for space. I *am* the space. I do not need to be invited to the table. I am carving my own. I have turned survival into strategy. Scar tissue into blueprints. Invisible pain into visible impact.

I am not the exception. I am the example. Of what is possible. Of what is next. I wear crowns and cannulas. I laugh loudly. I lead softly. I rest intentionally. I am not powerful because I perform well... I am powerful because I am still *here*. So let the world adjust. Let the walls fall. Let the light in. Because I was made for this. And I am by grace and by fire.

UNSTOPPABLE. CUT TO CREDITS.

About the Author

Juliet Romeo is a filmmaker, storyteller, and mentor who has made it her mission to lead by example and build platforms for others to rise. As the creator of Unstoppable at the Slamdance Film Festival, she pioneered a movement that has opened doors for disabled filmmakers and made inclusion a central part of the indie film conversation. With a background in journalism and years of experience mentoring emerging artists, Juliet brings clarity, authenticity, and fierce advocacy into every classroom, writer's room, and festival panel.

Her award-winning films have aired on PBS and Delta Airlines, and her passion for storytelling continues to inspire the next generation of creatives. Juliet lives in South Florida with her husband—a U.S. Army veteran—and their two Yorkies, Cooper and Pom Pom. Whether she's mentoring new talent or standing boldly in rooms not built for her, Juliet leads with heart, wisdom, and an unshakable commitment to helping others find and share their voice.

Acknowledgements

To my Mother, Jennifer—my ride-or-die, my truth-teller, and the original Trini firecracker, who never missed a beat when it came to pushing me. You've been lovingly, aggressively, and consistently in my ear: "Write the book already, Juliet!" So, I did. For you. Thank you for always believing in me, even when I doubted myself. You're a phenomenal mother, and if I grow into half the woman you are—I've already won.

To my nieces—Kristin, Megan, and Nia—my beautiful little trailblazers. You keep me on my toes and remind me every day that representation matters. You're my little shadows, my inspiration, my living proof that Black girl excellence runs in the family. Watching your eyes light up when I win reminds me that the next generation is always watching. Auntie is doing this for you. Walk like you own every room, because you do.

To my baby sisters—Amanda, we're one step closer, and girl, we're just getting started. Jezra, my twin flame with a twist—you already know. Our path is lined with purpose, and I'm so grateful to walk it beside you both.

To my tribe of girlfriends, my soul sisters, and my besties who cheer for me like I'm Beyoncé's understudy at Coachella—thank you. We hold each other up, laugh until we cry, and dream out loud together. Blood couldn't make us any closer, and I wouldn't want to do life without y'all.

To my grandmother, Jemma Romeo—who named me like a prophecy and walked this earth with wisdom, pride, and resilience. You crossed oceans with nothing but a vision and look at the legacy now. I am your dream realized, and I feel your hand guiding mine every time I write my name.

To every mentor, professor, fellowship director, and sickle cell advocate who poured into me—thank you for seeing something in me and fanning the flame. Your words, your guidance, and your belief helped mold the leader I am. This book? This moment? This mission? You're in the blueprint.

To the ones I've lost along the way, to the pain that has tried to stop me, and to the faith that has kept me moving—I honor all of it. I lead because I've been led. I rise because I've fallen. And I share this story because I know it will spark someone else's breakthrough.

The Force Behind the Storm: Kebra C. Moore, Visionary

Kebra C. Moore is a No. 1 Amazon bestselling author of four compelling novels, the founder and CEO of Welcome To The Storm Publishing, and the visionary behind the powerful anthology series, Our Power – The Anthology. A passionate advocate, creator, and entrepreneur, Kebra uses every platform available to uplift and amplify the voices of women who are too often overlooked—especially those within the disability community.

A graduate of Claflin University, Kebra earned her degree in Music Education and has long blended her love for the arts with her commitment to advocacy. She is also an accomplished singer-songwriter; her original song *"He'll Make a Way"* was featured in the documentary *Becoming Barack*, chronicling the early life of President Barack Obama.

After surviving a life-altering spinal cord injury, Kebra made the decision to transform her pain into purpose. She realized that far too many stories from women with disabilities, particularly Black women, were being silenced or forgotten. Determined to change that, she launched *Our Power – The Anthology*, a collection built to showcase real, raw, and resilient voices from across the country.

The first volume, *Our Power – The Anthology: Melanated Queens Rising Beyond Disabilities*, was released in March 2025 and brought together powerful stories of survival and triumph from women who continue to defy the odds. It was followed by Volume II in July 2025, titled *Our Power – The Anthology: Four Women. Four Journeys. One Powerful Collection*, which highlighted the unique paths and shared strength of four extraordinary contributors. The series will continue with Volume III, *Our Power – The Anthology: Women in Leadership*, set for release in October 2025, centering the experiences of women who lead with grace, grit, and purpose despite the obstacles they face.

Outside of publishing, Kebra is the creator of the Tropical Storm Collection, a vibrant beauty line known for its bestselling matte lipsticks and the highly anticipated *Sunset Shades* eyeshadow palette. Her goal with every product is to help women feel bold, beautiful, and seen.

Kebra has been married for over 25 years and is the proud mother of two grown sons. She is also an active and financial member of Delta Sigma Theta Sorority, Incorporated, through which she continues to mentor, serve, and support communities in need.

In January 2026, Kebra will expand her mission even further by launching an 8-week course titled *"Start Your Own Publishing Company,"* where she will guide aspiring entrepreneurs through the fundamentals of building a fast-paced, sustainable publishing business—from forming an LLC and securing ISBNs, to formatting, distribution, marketing, and beyond.

Her journey is one of resilience, purpose, and undeniable power. Through every storm, she has found a way not just to survive—but to lead, create, and elevate others along the way.

To learn more about publishing your book or enrolling in Kebra's 8-week course, visit w2tspublishing.org.